GO

● An all-colour guide packed with information for the young cyclist

CYCLING

Ken Evans

HAMLYN

Acknowledgments

Illustrations by Industrial Art Studio, St Ives.
The illustration on page 46 is reproduced from 'Which' by permission of the Publisher – The Consumers' Association.
The following illustrations have been adapted from material loaned by Mary Evans Picture Library, London 22–3, 28 top, 29 bottom, 31, 33; Historical Picture Service, Brentwood 23; Science Museum, London 24–5 bottom.

Photographs

Allsport/J. Pierce 153 bottom left; Allsport/Vandystadt 153 bottom right, Jean Marc Barey 114–15, 146–7, Gerard Vandystadt 66; A.P.I.S., Paris 26 bottom right; J. Allan Cash, London 5, 6, 7 centre, 10 bottom; Neville Chanin 10 top and centre, 17 centre, 20, 72, 105 bottom, 106, 108; Colorsport, London 113, 126, 131, 135 bottom, 141, 142–3, 148, 149 top and centre, 150 bottom, 151, 153 top left; Controller of Her Majesty's Stationery Office 80; Cycling Magazine, Sutton 94, 111, 126–7, 128, 128–9, 130–1, 138, 138–9; Mary Evans Picture Library, London 24, 26 top left, top right, centre right and bottom left, 27 bottom, 32 centre and bottom; 'Freewheel', London 11, 49, 73 top and bottom, 74 bottom, 83, 96–7, 136; Derek Hall 54; Hamlyn Group – John Howard 13 bottom, 14 top and bottom, 15, 16 top and bottom, 18, 21 bottom, 42, 52–3, 56–7, 57, 60–1, 62–3, 68–9, 74 top, 82, 98, 99, David Spurdens 8–9, 38, 40 top and bottom, 41 (all three), 50 (all three), 51, 132–3; Historical Picture Service, Brentwood 7 top; Audrey Hughes 117; Tim Hughes 13 top, 17 bottom, 19, 21 top, 27 top, 70 top and bottom, 93, 95 bottom, 100–1, 102–3, 105 top, 109, 110–11, 122–3, 124, 125 top and bottom, 137, 144–5, 149 bottom, 152; London Cycling Campaign 17 top; Mansell Collection, London 24–5 top, 26 centre left, 28 bottom, 32 top left and top right, 35, 36, 118–19; Leo Mason 120–1, 153 top right and centre; Alex Moulton Limited, Bradford on Avon 55, 71, 95 top, 112, 116, 119, 120, 140; Raleigh, Nottingham 4–5, 67, 135 top; Spectrum Colour Library, London 7 bottom, 78; Temple Press, London 29; Youth Hostels Association 101.

The Publishers acknowledge with thanks the assistance of the following: Feltham Road Club, E. Chamberlaine & Son Ltd., Ken Ryall Cycles and Geoff Elder.

Front jacket: Top: Allsport/Vandystadt. Bottom: HGPL
Back jacket: HGPL

This edition first published in 1987 by
The Hamlyn Publishing Group Limited
Bridge House, 69 London Road, Twickenham, Middlesex.

ISBN: 0 600 53175 9

Printed in Hong Kong by Mandarin Offset

First published 1979 as *The Young Cyclist's Handbook*
This edition revised and reset

CONTENTS

INTRODUCTION

The bicycle is such a simple means of getting around that it's surprising it took so long to be invented. You sit on the saddle, press down on the pedals and you're moving, with little more energy than you use walking, and a lot more speed.

Since a strange two-wheeled wooden machine first made its appearance in Paris in 1791, the bicycle has undergone many changes, and from being a curiosity it has become a cheap and efficient means of transport, a healthy outdoor pursuit, a beast of burden and – sometimes – a symbol of status. Cycling is a sport for thousands and a pleasure for millions. Without the bicycle the world would be a different place.

Happily, many countries have, for different reasons, recognized that the bicycle has a special place in their society.

Flat countries are ideal for cycling and in such areas it is naturally a very popular means of transport. In the Netherlands for

example much has been done to help the large number of cyclists get around easily, especially in towns. There are special cycle

paths everywhere, either as marked-off lanes on normal roads, or taking completely different routes from one point to another. Sometimes busy junctions with motor roads are completely avoided; elsewhere traffic lights include a special phase so that cycles can manoeuvre without hindrance from other traffic.

Another country where the bicycle is a major form of transport is China. There the motor car is comparatively scarce, and cycling is the most convenient available alternative.

Even the rickshaw, the oriental equivalent of the taxi, has pressed bicycling into service, so that the seated passenger is drawn along,

▷ Flat roads in the
Netherlands mean
easy cycling.

A 'pedi-cab' in Patna, India.

not by a runner between the shafts of the carriage, but by a cyclist.

In many countries the bicycle often carries not only a rider but a great deal of merchandise as well.

In the 1914-18 War there were bicycle battalions in some armies, and in the 1939-45 War collapsible bicycles were dropped along with parachute troops.

Even more recently, bicycles were used by North Vietnamese troops for long-distance equipment movement on jungle trails impassable to motor vehicles.

In many African states the sturdy 'roadster', with its heavy frame, oil-bath gearcase and flat handlebars, is a prize possession, costing sometimes many weeks' pay to an unskilled worker. Its role is again as a personal means of transport and a luggage carrier, on roads which are often little more than tracks.

The bicycle occupies a different position in the United States of America. Since the 'bike boom' of the early 1970s, Americans have literally taken the bicycle to their hearts. Worries about heart attacks made businessmen think of taking exercise. Problems of fuel supply made other citizens leave their cars in the garage and pedal to work. Families discovered that they could enjoy the countryside together using bicycles. And those concerned with the environment, and preserving the countryside, pointed out that cycling is quiet and does not pollute the atmosphere – unlike, of course, the internal combustion engine.

There were rallies in American cities, asking for safe facilities for commuting cyclists, as a result of which many authorities created cycle lanes on highways, and others closed certain streets to motor traffic, calling them 'bike routes'.

▷ Italian riflemen 1915. The bicycle even has a use in wartime.

▷ Beast of burden – the bicycle helps farmers in Peking.

▷ Special cycle paths in Stevenage, England, underpassing other roads.

Many other states went further. Taking into account the vast increase in the number of pleasure cyclists, they introduced the 'bike trail', sometimes routed along minor roads, sometimes along easily-ridable paths, but always reserved for cyclists wanting to enjoy the scenic beauty of an area.

When Americans celebrated the 200th anniversary of the founding of their country, the bicycle was part of it: a 'Bikecentennial' brought cyclists from many countries to follow a coast-to-coast route, using designated bike trails wherever possible, and staying in hostels, schools and local homes.

In Britain the best facilities for day-to-day cycling were provided when Stevenage New Town in Hertfordshire was designed. A now flourishing trading estate and the town itself were connected and criss-crossed by a network of cycle paths which avoided roads where possible, by using underpasses and flyovers. This scheme, because it was part of an original town-planning concept, has been highly successful over years of usage and in Stevenage many more people use bicycles for shopping and getting to work than in most British towns.

In the 1980s many cities have shown more concern for the needs of cyclists, setting up special lanes on roads which can only be used by cyclists, sometimes with special junctions and even traffic lights where these lanes cross busy roads. In other cases, routes have been signposted which avoid the most dangerous roads. Some cities have also installed special cycle parks, with locking racks so that you can park your cycle tidily and safely.

Some attempts to aid cycling in towns have failed, however, mainly because they gave the bicycle priority, but not exclusive use, of certain roads parallel to main thoroughfares. It just isn't enough to guarantee the cyclist safety and a smooth passage, and somehow the pressure of a car-oriented society is too much to keep these experimental schemes going for long.

Another major contribution has been to give cyclists the use of 'bus lanes' in London and some other cities, allowing them to breeze past traffic jams without trouble.

Cycle racing is one of the most popular sports in Europe, with the front pages of French newspapers devoted to the Tour de France, the world's biggest professional event.

France, Italy, Belgium and Holland are the world's major cycle racing countries, where a talented cyclist can make his fortune.

There are many cycle racing tracks, some of which are indoors. Even in the depths of winter cross-country cycling

▷ The BMX has brought the thrills of cycle racing to kids from six upwards.

All-weather transport: enthusiasts tackle snow in the USA.

fans can practise cyclo-cross or mountain-bike racing: ride your bike if you can, carry it or push it when you can't.

For BMX fanatics, there are racing circuits and BMX parks where you can develop your stunting technique, working out new acrobatic routines or going for broke with sky-high leaps.

Mountain-bikers love the challenge of taking their steeds to places where no one has ever ventured with a bike before, even if it means hauling it half the way on a rope up a sheer rock face.

Then there is bicycle polo, cycle-ball, and 'artistic' cycling (a kind of acrobatic show on wheels). In Japan track racing draws enormous crowds, and its riders are paid fortunes from the proceeds of betting, rather like horse-racing in many other countries.

Apart from racing there are so many uses to which a cycle can be put: ask the postman, the mobile ice-cream man and the newspaper delivery boy.

Put paddles on a cycle instead of wheels and you have the makings of a pedal-boat. Connect it up properly and the stationary

bike can become a power generator. And perhaps the most significant advance came in 1979, when a team of American designers put wings on a bicycle and it flew the English Channel.

On a bicycle, the sky's the limit!

The pedalling ice-cream man.

Cycling acrobats in China.

Mountain bikes, or all-terrain bikes, can take you anywhere in comfort and style.

WHY CYCLE?

Cycling saves money, it's healthy, it's quick and convenient, and it helps the world stay a nice place to be in. Cycling is both an exciting sport and an interesting recreation – and you can make lots of new friends through cycling.

Viewed like that, it's a wonder cycling isn't more popular than it is. But cycling, as a sport and pastime, *is* becoming more popular for all these reasons – and because modern manufacturers have taken the 'push' out of the 'push-bike'. Today's bicycles are easier to ride, better designed, attractive to look at – and lots of fun.

Cycling saves money

A new bicycle could cost as little as £100, or it could cost more than ten times that much, if you want a bicycle to win a world championship! Buying a second-hand bicycle is, of course, one of the cheapest ways to start your cycling career. Once you have your machine, what else is there to spend?

You need front and rear lights, run off either batteries or a dynamo, for riding at night. Then you need a good cycle lock, so you keep your bicycle safe from theft.

If they aren't already supplied, then you'll need a saddlebag and a simple tool kit, waterproof to keep out the wet, and you're all set.

Spare a thought for the car driver. He has to pay for insurance, plus a contribution towards the cost of keeping up the roads, before he can even start his car.

Then there's petrol, oil, plus the cost of regular services and difficult repairs. Being a motorist is an expensive business.

Take the cyclist in contrast. It's wise to take out an insurance on your bicycle in case it is stolen or damaged in an accident, but this needn't cost much. The cyclist can probably ride as far on a cup of tea as a car will travel on a gallon of petrol. Most repairs you can do yourself, in the garden shed. And if a cycle is well maintained, with regular oilings and greasings, then the only running expenses could turn out to be an occasional new tyre or inner tube.

Cycling is healthy

Cycling is healthy, but it needn't be strenuous. You can ride as fast as you want, or as slowly as you want, taking either vigorous exercise or just a gentle work-out. You can go out cycling for a whole day or more, or perhaps for a brief half-hour, and still enjoy the exercise.

Riding a bicycle is not just exercise for the legs, either. Pushing down on the pedals involves the important muscles of the lower back too. When the going gets harder, the arm and shoulder muscles get a lot of use. And all the time, your breathing

▷ Cycling is a
marvellous way to
enjoy the 'great
outdoors'.

is being improved by rhythmical exercise.

Only running and rowing are more complete exercises for the whole body – and they can be a lot more strenuous.

Cycling is recognized by most doctors as a good form of rehabilitation – getting your body used to normal life again after an illness or injury.

▷ A stationary 'keep-
fit' bicycle. Ideal
for use in health clubs.

Stationary cycles have their place in hospitals, where patients needing controlled exercise can pedal to their heart's content – even though they may not get very far!

Because body weight is supported partly by the saddle and handlebars, cycling is an important aid to recovery from leg, thigh and pelvis injuries, and pains in the lower back. In most cases, a patient can cycle to improve his leg strength before he can actually walk. Racing cyclists, recovering from a broken thigh, have even been known to get out on their bicycles – with crutches strapped to the crossbar just in case they have to spend a brief spell off the bicycle during their outing!

Modern thinking on recovery from heart attacks includes gentle cycling after a brief period of convalescence.

Statistics show that lifelong cyclists have fewer heart attacks, don't suffer so many breathing problems, and are generally fitter than their non-cycling neighbours.

Cycling is quick and convenient

Cycling makes life easy too. It's a simple matter to get your bicycle out and pop down to the shops or the youth club, not having to depend on a lift, a bus or train.

Bicycles can carry a fair amount of luggage. Some designed for long distance touring can be used to carry camping gear or enough clothes for weeks away; other machines are built to take specially designed bags on carriers, which are easily removable for shopping.

You can keep your bicycle in a garage, lean it against a wall or, if space is limited, hang it from a hook on the ceiling. There are folding bicycles which can be kept in a cupboard or under the stairs.

Folding bicycles all have small wheels but full-sized wheels on many machines have quick-release hubs. In a matter of seconds the wheels are out, and can be stored alongside the frame in a small space.

One of the welcome changes in bicycle construction over the past few years has been the introduction of bargain-priced accessories in alloy, previously too expensive for all but the dedicated cyclist.

Using alloy instead of steel components – for hubs, rims, handlebars, stems, chainwheels and gears can all be steel or alloy – means a lighter machine. A lighter machine is easier to pedal, will travel further on the same amount of effort – and if you need

◁ Even a conventional bicycle takes up little space, if you remove the wheels.

◁ Simple storage: two nails, and a bicycle is easily hung up on a wall.

Some bicycles fold up easily, and can fit into a car boot.

to, you can carry it upstairs much more easily.

The bicycles ridden at the turn of the century would weigh over 18 kilograms (40 pounds). Now an average sports bicycle will weigh around 12 kilograms (25 pounds) and racing cycles can be much less than 9 kilograms (20 pounds) in weight. So think how much easier cycling is for you than your counterpart of 80 years ago!

Cycling helps preserve our environment

Many responsible people in the latter half of this century have become worried about the environment – the state of the world we live in.

They are concerned about our natural energy resources, such as coal, gas and oil, being exhausted. They study the gradual pollution of our world: factories belching out grimy smoke into the atmosphere, car exhausts fogging the towns and cities, streams and rivers losing their

flow and their fish through being clogged with industrial waste. Noise levels, too, are worrying, from the near unbearable aircraft noise close to airports to the nagging and tension-producing drone of heavy traffic.

The bicycle has little part in all this. It needs a few drops of lubricating oil every so often, but otherwise the only resources it needs are physical ones – leg power. It doesn't pollute the atmosphere, doesn't make undue noise.

What's more, the bicycle helps you to enjoy to the full the sights of the countryside – or the city. There are no parking problems – just stop when and where you want, prop your bicycle against a wall or lay it down on a grass verge – remembering to lock it up securely and remove the pump and lights if you are going to leave it for any length of time.

You don't even have to stay on roads. Cycles may be ridden on bridle paths (though not on footpaths) and where you can't ride, bicycles can always be wheeled or carried.

Lightweight
bicycles can easily
be lifted over obstacles.

Riding along at a comfortable pace means you can take in much more of the passing countryside than from the window of a speeding car. And because your progress is quiet, you don't disturb other people or animals the way a motor vehicle does.

In town, travelling by bicycle is often as fast as using a car.

▷ Special crossings are used where cycle lanes cross other roads, with bollards to stop cars from taking the short cut.

△ Some countries have special scenic routes planned for cyclists. This one is in the USA and was made for the 1976 'Bikecentennial'.

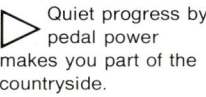

▷ Quiet progress by pedal power makes you part of the countryside.

Cycling is both a sport and a recreation

Cycling can make you a lot of new friends who share the same interest. At school there are always fellow enthusiasts who'll go cycling with you. Sometimes there are school cycling clubs and some forward-thinking schools even have cycling on the curriculum.

Cycling clubs

There are many cycling clubs, more than a thousand in Britain, and many more in other European countries, America, and wherever else cycling is popular.

Some cycling clubs specialize in racing, but the vast majority do everything connected with cycling. They will have a weekly club night, where members gather to discuss plans, talk about equipment, hear lectures or look at slides and films.

Another regular event, usually

17

The sociable side
of cycling: a typical
club run.

on Sunday mornings, is the club run, a steady ride to a set destination and back, making a whole day of it.

Stops for 'elevenses', lunch and tea encourage a social atmosphere, and mean that you don't get too tired by riding for a long time without a break. Generally a club run will cover between 80 and 160 kilometres (50-100 miles) depending on the terrain.

Joining a cycling club is a good first step towards becoming an experienced cyclist. Its members, of all ages, are usually happy to pass on their own knowledge, with tips on maintenance, riding style and selection of equipment.

Touring

Some clubs have flourishing touring sections, whose activities will feature weekend or longer tours at home or abroad, using youth hostels or other inexpensive accommodation. If there's one thing better than going on a cycling holiday, it's going on one with a group of other cyclists.

When you get more experienced in planning tours, you might want to 'rough it' and go cycle camping. Modern materials mean camping equipment can be bought which is light and compact, and one person (or better, two) can carry full camping gear on a bicycle with careful planning and packing. More about this later.

You may not fancy the idea of touring with full camping gear weighing you down, or you may be doubtful about touring on your own in an area you haven't visited before. There are now people who can help you out. They offer organized tours, camping or inexpensive accom-

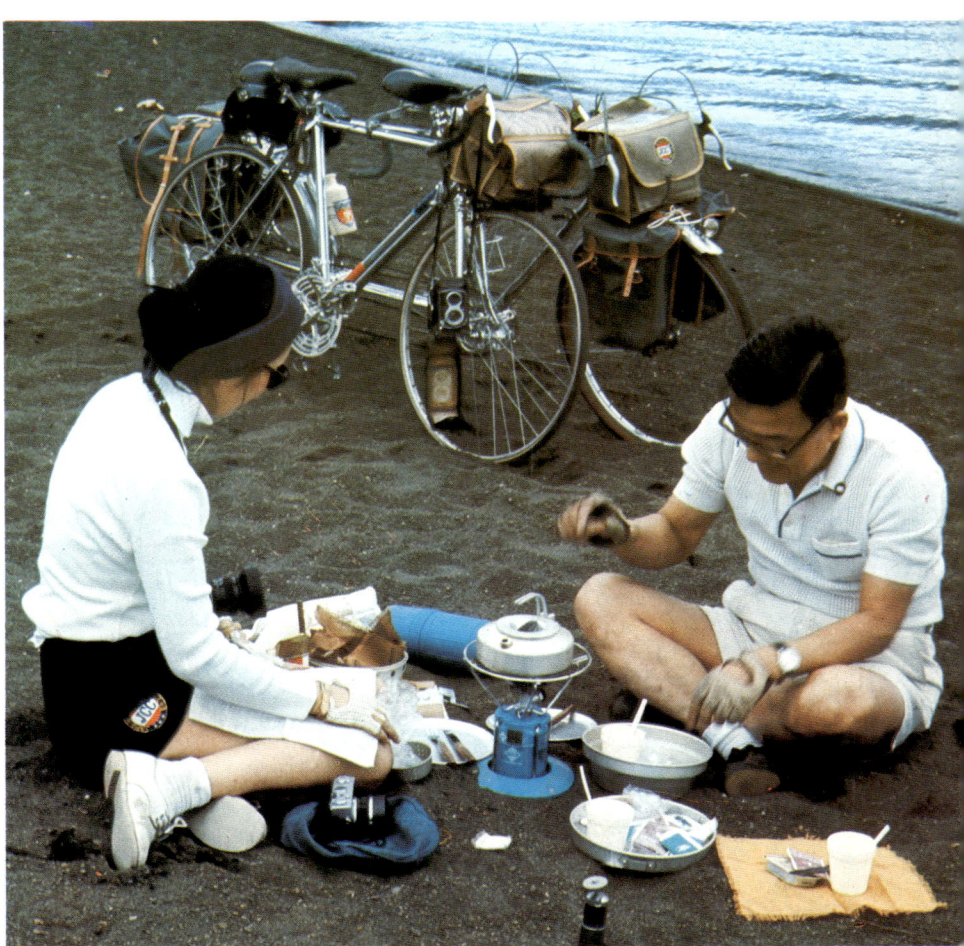

You can carry your kitchen with you on a bicycle.

modation, and they make sure there is a hot dinner waiting for you in the evening and a big breakfast before you set out next morning. Each day rides are planned, though you do not have to ride with everyone else if you don't want to. Some of these tours even have a van that carries all your luggage, driven by a mechanic ready to leap out and help you mend your puncture or straighten your buckled wheel. Cycle touring made easy!

You might prefer something a little more competitive than ordinary cycle touring, and there are lots of ways to compete – without actually racing.

Reliability trials

Most clubs run reliability trials, usually in the late winter and early spring. These consist of riding round a pre-set course within a set time, perhaps 160 kilometres (100 miles) in 8 hours, or 80 kilometres (50 miles) in $3\frac{1}{2}$ hours.

If there is a manageable entry, all the riders set off together, but a large entry means a number of groups being sent off at intervals.

As the name suggests, the aim is to test reliability, not speed. Many riders would find averaging 20 kph ($12\frac{1}{2}$ mph) an easy matter; others might find it a challenge. But reliability trials are prevented from turning into all-out 'blinds' by a rule which stops riders reaching the finish more than a certain time (usually 15 to 30 minutes) before their target time.

Tourist rides

In France this reliability trial system is extended over much longer distances. They have rides for *brevets* (diplomas) which witness that the rider has ridden from, say, Dunkirk to Menton within a stated time.

The French have a number of famous 'diagonal' routes which criss-cross their country and all have their diplomas.

It's a very much more serious form of cycle touring than the humble club run, and demands much greater organization. On these long distance rides many clubs have support cars carrying food and spare clothing. Stops are arranged where riders can grab a bite to eat and snatch an hour or two of sleep.

Most famous of the tourist rides in France, attracting hundreds of participants, (and following the route of a now defunct race) is Paris-Brest-Paris, from the French capital to the Brittany port and back, a distance of about 1200 kilometres (750 miles).

There are several different organizations governing this kind of tourist riding in France, with various sets of rules. One might stipulate a set pace for its rides. Another demands that every rider's machine should be in tourist condition – that is carrying mudguards and a saddlebag.

Tourist trials

Similar in name, but different entirely, are tourist trials, organized widely, and including a national contest called the British Cycle Tourist Competition.

These require a rider to find his or her way round a countryside course, demonstrating map-reading ability. Contestants might be asked to cover a section of the course at a certain average speed (without the use of a watch, to test their judgement). At another point, a judge might pop out from behind a hedge to ask a question about the countryside, or to test observation. Another section might have to be covered without putting foot to earth – and negotiating muddy paths and stream crossings isn't that easy.

You may want to race seriously, but that's another story – which will be dealt with later.

Does cycling have any disadvantages?

Having heard about all the advantages – what about the disadvantages of cycling?

When you tell your friends that you cycle, you might hear one say: 'that's too much like hard work for me!' Or another might bring up the problems of riding in the cold or wet.

Tourist trials test your knowledge of the countryside, as well as testing your bike-handling ability.

▷ The worst of weather needn't stop you cycling if you dress sensibly. Pedalling will keep you warm.

▷ A rainsuit is useful for wet weather cycling. Always carry your rain gear with you.

Neither need worry you much. For a start, cycling is as hard as you make it.

Of course you can turn it into hard work if you want to, either on purpose, by going out with the aim of exhausting yourself, or because of plain ignorance or obstinacy, trying to hump the bicycle along in top gear when conditions aren't favourable. Modern design and construction means cycles are for pleasure riding, not torture!

In bad weather, the principle is the same as walking – you wrap up to suit the conditions. You can wear a cape, leggings, shoe-spats and sou'wester as traditional protection against the rain, or you can buy a modern rain-suit, which is a lot less complicated and a lot more comfortable.

The temperature needs to be well below freezing before, adequately clad, you'll feel cold on a bicycle. The exercise of turning the pedals is generally enough to keep the blood flowing nicely. And don't forget all the fares you save, all the exercise you're getting, all the new friends you're making, won't that give you a nice warm feeling?

THE HISTORY OF THE BICYCLE

The common bicycle of today seems such a simple machine. Two wheels, held in a frame, a saddle to sit on, handlebars giving direct steering. Turning pedals attached to cranks sends the propulsion to the rear wheel by a narrow chain. And there's your easy mode of travel, without worrying about refinements like different gearing, super-light materials, or aerodynamics.

Yet it has taken nearly two centuries for the bicycle to develop from its forerunners, and about a hundred years were needed before evolution and experiment produced the first machine which closely resembled the bicycle we ride today.

The first bicycle

In 1791 in the gardens of the Royal Palace, Paris, onlookers saw the young Comte de Sivrac, known as an inventor by some and regarded as an eccentric by others, astride a strange machine of wood.

It had two wheels of moderate

size and a crossbar on which the rider sat, holding on to a carved horse's head where now the handlebars would be. The whole strange machine was made of wood and must have been very heavy.

De Sivrac called it the 'Célérifère', a machine of speed. He propelled it by scooting along with each leg in turn. Most laughed at the novelty, but among the young bloods of the fashionable Parisian society the invention quickly gained popularity. By 1793 it was known as the Vélocifère. The British called it the Hobby-horse or Dandy-horse.

The Draisiènne of the early 1820s.

Steering

In 1817 a forestry inspector in Germany, Baron von Drais de Sauerbrun, created his own version of the Vélocifère, which could be steered by turning the head, whereas its predecessor could be directed only by leaning in the required direction.

This modification of the original idea became known as the Draisiènne, and in 1818 a coach-maker called Denis Johnson started to make them in Britain, under licence. But they were still uncomfortable and tiring. Bad roads, and the iron treads on the wooden wheels, meant a bumpy ride for anyone who rode the new contraptions.

Driving the wheels

In 1839 a Scottish blacksmith from Courthill in Dumfries and Galloway, Kirkpatrick Macmillan, produced a 'Vélocipède' which wasn't driven by the scooting action of feet on the road but by a drive mechanism to the rear wheel. It meant that, for the first time, a two-wheeled machine was able to be propelled by leg-power without feet touching the ground.

Instead, the rider's feet were on treadles (like those used on an old-fashioned sewing machine).

It took Paris by storm in the 1790s: the Célérifère of the Comte de Sivrac.

These were linked by long rods to the rear wheel; by pushing forward on each treadle alternately, the rear wheel was turned. And with this invention came the discovery that man could balance on a two-wheeled machine, and that its very forward motion, the 'gyroscopic effect' of the wheels, made balancing more and more easy as speed increased. Even so, the fact that the ride was not very comfortable is recalled by the Vélocipède's nickname of 'Boneshaker'.

The pneumatic tyre

In 1845 came another invention which was to make cycling far more popular. Again the inventor was Scottish, an engineer called Robert Thomson. He invented

▷ Learning to ride a Draisiènne at Johnson's riding school, London, in 1819.

▷ Macmillan and his Vélocipède, the first bicycle with a drive mechanism to the rear wheel.

and patented a tyre, made up of an inflated rubber tube and a leather cover – not for bicycles, however, but for the great horse-drawn carts and carriages with which he worked. Only four decades later was his invention applied to bicycles.

Pedals

Meanwhile bicycle design took another direction. In 1861 a French coachmaker called Pierre Michaux took in an old Hobby-horse for repair at his Paris works. In a flash of inspiration, he decided to try to improve on the existing machine by extending the hub into cranks each side – 'like the crank handle on a grind stone' – one of his sons, Henry, later recounted. The other son, Ernest, put the idea into practice,

Some unusual bicycles

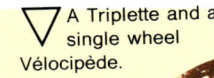
A Triplette and a single wheel Vélocipède.

The 'Invincible' tandem and a bicycle railway.

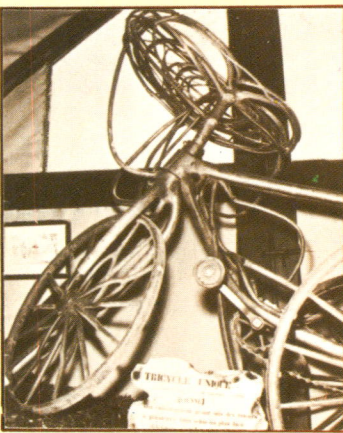

A bicycle 'omnibus' and a tricycle that took ten years to 'grow'.

An original Michaux Vélocipède, ridden by an enthusiast at a rally of historic bicycles.

and the first bicycle driven by pedals and cranks took shape.

It meant that the rider had a direct method of driving the front wheel. With one revolution of the cranks, the wheel turned once, and the machine covered a distance determined by the diameter of the front wheel.

The new 'pedal-driven Vélocipède' quickly became commercialized, and by 1866 a former employee of Michaux, Pierre Lallement, had gone to America and taken out a patent there. Meanwhile the Michaux family set about improving their original, looking for better materials, using a spring mounting for the saddle to give much needed comfort, and adding a cord-tightened brake which pressed down on the front wheel – altogether a better way of stopping than putting both feet down and watching the sparks fly.

The first bicycle race, held in Paris in 1868.

◁ Easily recognisable even now, the Penny-Farthing or Ordinary bicycle. Its gearing was limited by the size of the front wheel.

The Penny-Farthing

Some logical changes came about because more speed was wanted by the devotees. Naturally there was a limit to the number of times a man could pedal every minute, so to increase the speed the size of the front driving wheel was altered – the bigger the wheel, the faster the speed, until the rider reached the limit of his leg length.

As the front wheel got bigger, so the rear wheel became smaller, and what we call the 'Penny-Farthing' was developed, with a front wheel about twice the size of today's standard wheels. The tiny wheel trailed along happily behind, doing little more than helping with stability. The machine was nicknamed the Penny-Farthing after two British coins in

◁ A team of Penny-Farthing riders in 1872.

An early cycle show in London.

circulation at that time – the tiny farthing and the much larger, old-fashioned penny.

Mounting the machine was an acquired art. You could take the easy way and lean it against a wall while you climbed on (via an iron step which stuck out from the side of the frame), or you could put one foot on that same step, scoot with the other to get things moving, then vault into the saddle – rather like a cowboy mounting a moving horse.

Although we call it a Penny-Farthing, it was originally only a developing version of the Vél-ocipède (which the British had called the 'Boneshaker'). At the time it was known as the 'High Wheeler', and later, more simply, as the 'Ordinary'.

It provided a different kind of ride to the Boneshaker, which

Mounting a Penny-Farthing.

was not very fast, and rattled its way over the uneven road surfaces.

The high-wheeled machine gave the impression of floating over uneven surfaces, and because of his height above the ground, the rider felt automatically superior. He could go faster too, and 'racers' developed a distinctive style of leaning forward over the front wheel while their legs whirled around.

There was one major drawback, apart from the problem of mounting: if the machine hit a brick or large stone, the rider was quite often catapulted forward over the front wheel, frequently injuring himself quite badly.

Later improvements to the Boneshaker, such as iron rims, wire spokes which could be tightened to correct any buckling of the wheel, solid rubber tyres and ball bearings, were all incorporated into the 'Ordinary'. Ball bearings lessened friction on the hub and pedal axles.

Chain drive

While the Ordinary design was in full swing, experiments in chain drive were taking place – experiments which, by 1890, were to outdate the tall stately machine which had done so much to popularize cycling.

In 1875 an Englishman from Gloucester, George Shergold, built a bicycle where the drive came from cranks, via a continuous chain, to the rear wheel. Kirkpatrick Macmillan's design of almost 40 years earlier was emerging once again.

The Bicyclette

In 1879 H. J. Lawson patented his Bicyclette (bicyclette is still the French word for bicycle), and the following year it was on the stand of the Tangent Bicycle Company at the Stanley Show. This really was an advance, although owing

▽ The Bicyclette of H. J. Lawson, which in 1879 took up Macmillan's principles.

The Rover Safety, a development of Lawson's machine, which caused the downfall of the Penny-Farthing. It was safer, and it could be easily geared to go faster.

much to Macmillan and also to the 1875 machine of Shergold.

The Bicyclette had a front wheel of just over 100 centimetres (40 inches) in diameter (smaller than on the average Ordinary), with a 61 centimetre (24 inch) rear wheel, which was larger than that in use on the Ordinary.

Its main frame tube ran from the steering head back to the rear forks, and from this tube hung down another, at the end of which was a chainwheel and cranks, with a chain leading to a sprocket on the rear hub.

The diamond frame

Lawson's Bicyclette was called the Safety, and several models were built, the most successful in 1885. Its main feature (apart from chain drive, of course) was the 'diamond' frame. This meant it had four main sets of tubes forming a diamond shape: the crossbar from the base of the saddle to the steering head; then the down tube from head to the bottom brackets (where the axle for the chainwheel was located); the chain stays from bottom bracket to either side of the rear hub; and the seat stays, from the rear hub back upwards to the saddle again. The forks each side of the front wheel came from the steering head joint, and the diamond was strengthened by a tube from saddle base to the bottom bracket, originally curved but later straight.

The Ordinary still had enormous support among the speed-seekers, but that support started to wane as Safety machines produced fast times, helped by the fact that a rear wheel drive (as the Safety was) could be geared far more easily than a front wheel drive (as the Ordinary was).

31

The virtual end of the Ordinary era was signalled when in 1888 John Boyd Dunlop, a Belfast veterinary surgeon, made a new kind of cushioned rubber tyre for his son's cycle. It was an inflatable rubber tube, enclosed by a canvas cover, which in turn had a tough rubber tread. The whole thing was stuck onto the wheel rim.

He patented it, and went into business with Harvey Du Cros in the Pneumatic Tyre Company in Dublin – only to discover, two years later, that his patent wasn't valid, since Robert Thomson, way back in 1845, had established the principle. The company saved itself by taking out another patent, that of securing the tyre by two wires which hooked under overhanging parts of the rim.

Whatever the patent situation, the pneumatic tyre was the making of the Safety bicycle. The chief advantage of the high-wheeled Ordinary, the way it coped with rough surfaces, was more than matched by the way the pneumatic tyre 'gave' as it rode over bumps or into ruts. On the Safety machine the rider was closer to the ground and didn't have so far to fall in case of an accident. His weight was more evenly distributed and he was more stable. Finally, the Safety machine, by changing the ratio of teeth on the chainwheel and on the rear-hub sprocket, had a greater possible gear range.

Brakes

Some developments dictated others. For instance, whereas a spoon-type brake operated by pressing down on the front tyre was quite acceptable when that tyre was solid rubber, it certainly didn't suit the pneumatic tyre, which quickly found its protective tread worn away. At the beginning of the 20th century

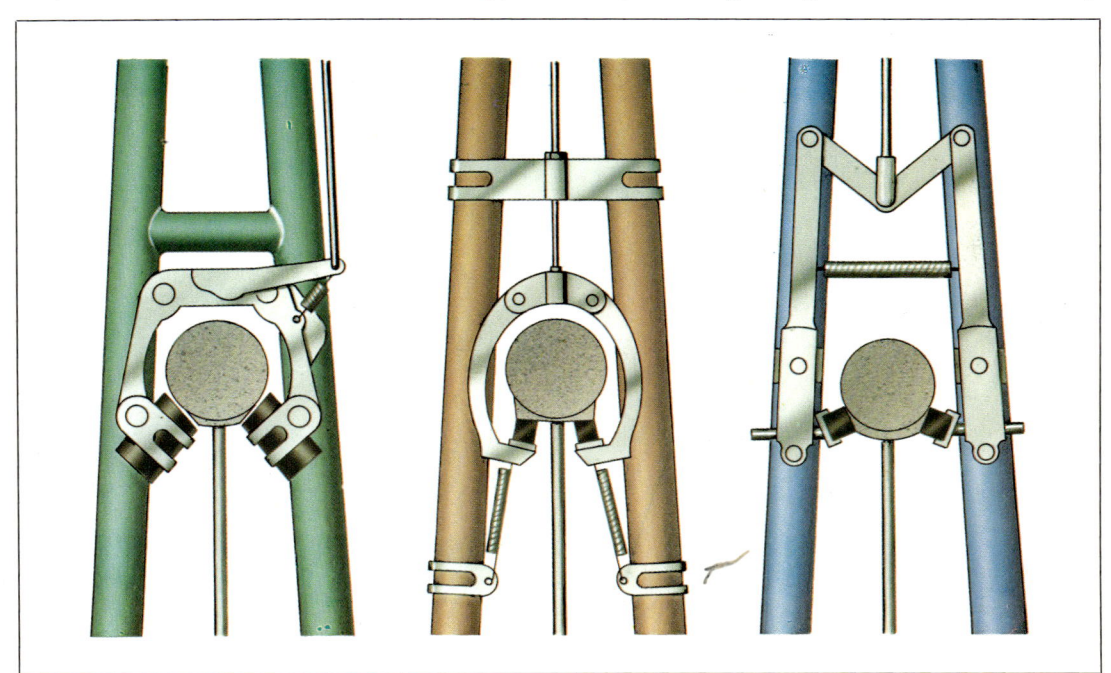

▽ Three different types of early rim brake. From left to right: the Dunois, the Bowden, and the Floquart. They incorporate principles which are still used today.

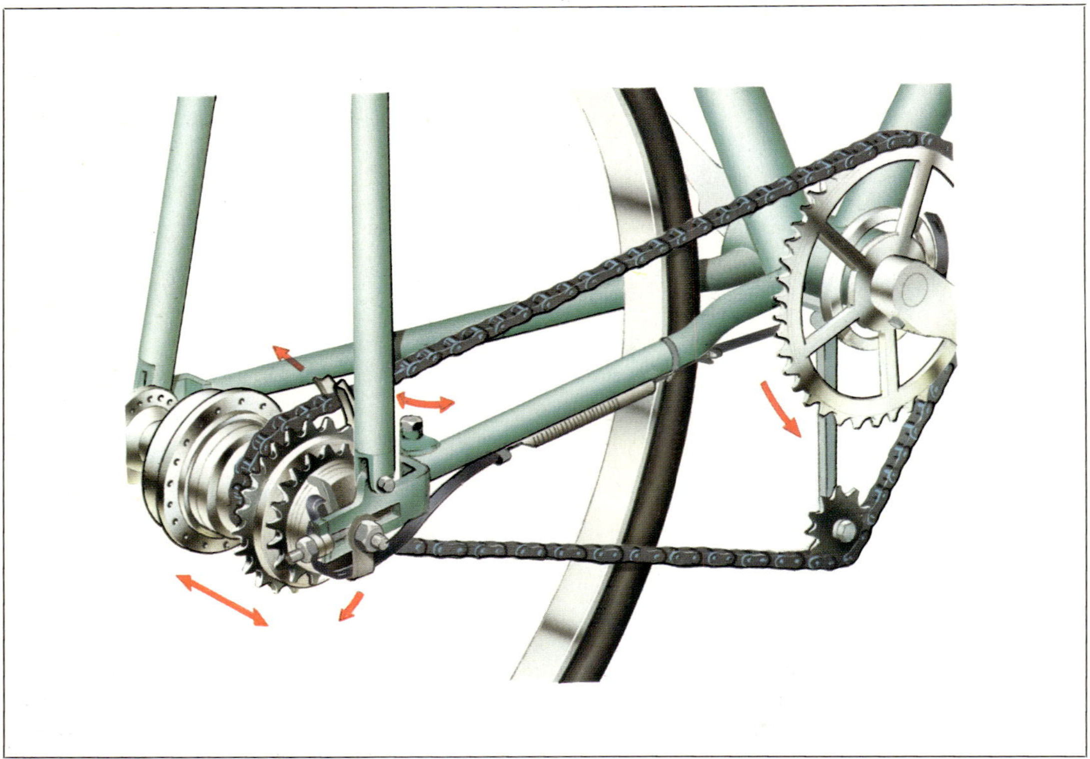

brakes were invented where a rubber shoe pressed on to the side of the rim, and later systems were introduced to slow a wheel at the hub.

The need for good brakes was made even more imperative by the invention, towards the end of the 19th century, of a freewheel, which meant that even though the rear wheel was going round, the cranks did not need to revolve and the pedals could be kept in one position. Descending steep hills became less of a problem (previously the rider had either had to flail his legs round at an enormous rate or take his feet off the pedals completely). But the freewheel removed the braking possibility which the fixed wheel offered – simply easing back on the pedals with a 'fixed' was a natural way of slowing down.

Gears

Another way of making cycling easier was the fitting of variable gears – after all, you don't want to ride up a hill in the same gear as you go down it.

There are two types of variable gears these days: the derailleur gear, with which the chain is derailed from one size of rear sprocket to another (anything between three and six sprockets is common, and even seven is possible), and the hub gear, an enclosed mechanism on the rear

The Gradient derailleur of 1899. A spring plate at the chainwheel is pulled round when back-pedalling. This operates two quadrant forks which pull the chain clear of the sprockets. These can be moved in either direction to engage a different gear. On pedalling forwards, the chain then drops back in place.

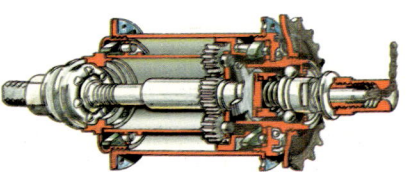

The Sturmey-Archer hub gear, whose design hasn't changed for years.

Two cyclists just before the turn of the century. The bicycle frame had become, by then, much more like that of a modern machine.

hub, working in a similar way to a car gearbox, with different sizes of cog-wheels meshing to create larger or smaller gear ratios.

Early versions of the derailleur gear – universally used by road racing riders now – appeared in the last decade of the 19th century. The hub gear was invented at about the same time. The most famous of the hub gears, the Sturmey-Archer, still popular today for leisure and roadster cycles, was introduced in 1902 by the Raleigh Cycle Company. This Nottingham-based firm was to become the world's biggest bicycle manufacturer. The inventors of the hub gear were Henry Sturmey and James Archer, whose joint work was snapped up by Raleigh. Their 'three-speed' followed engineering principles which have never needed to be changed.

Materials

While the shape of the frame, the basic diamond, changed little as the 20th century progressed, its materials did. Midland British companies such as Accles & Pollock and Reynolds Tube produced stronger frame tubing, with which thinner gauges could be used. The humble bicycle in this way used materials developed for some Second World War aircraft. Research done during the war also helped hasten the development of aluminium alloys, so that bicycle components such as chainwheels, wheel-rims and hubs, pedals, handlebars and extensions, could forsake the weight of steel for the lightness, and often similar strength, of appropriate alloys.

Tyres

Racing tyres developed too, with the production of a 'tubular' – a tyre not of separate inner tube and outer cover, but of the two combined. The unit could be stuck to a special rim with heavy glue, replacing the wired-on tyre of early years. The tubular could

John Boyd Dunlop's son, and his bicycle with the first pneumatic tyres (1888).

be pulled off the rim and a fresh one fitted in a couple of minutes, and any punctures mended when more time was available. Tubulars are used by almost every racing cyclist nowadays, even though the wired-on tyre retains its popularity with the 'bread-and-butter' cyclist as high-pressure tyres have improved.

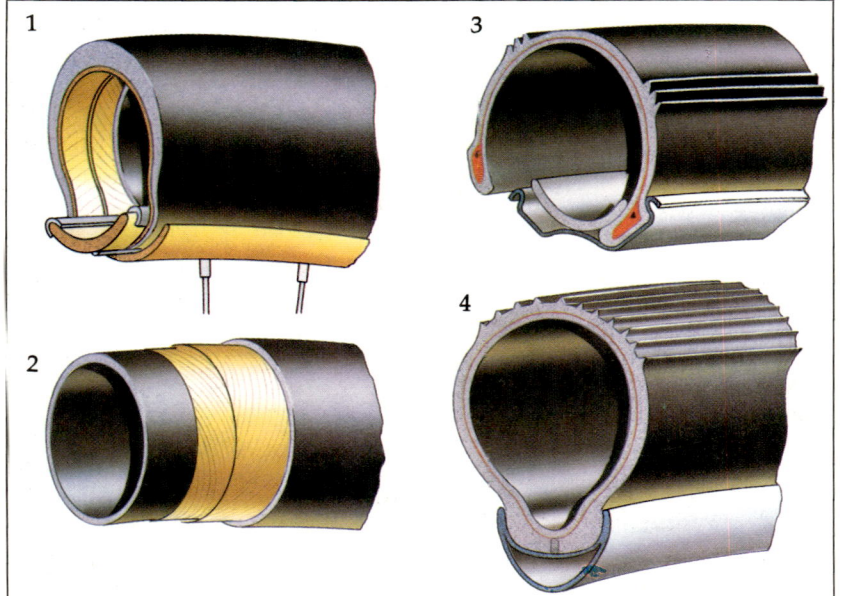

4 early pneumatic tyres: the original Dunlop invention, a cross ply development, the Clincher – which was the first attempt to key the cover to its rim with air pressure, and a tubeless design.

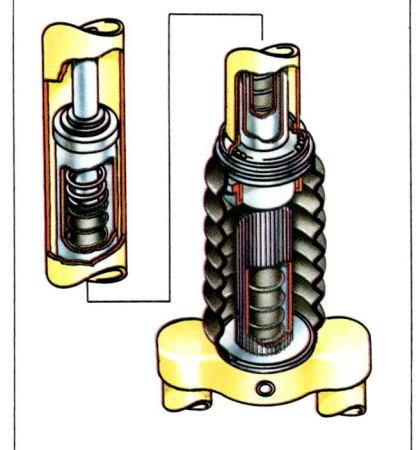

Recent developments

A major design change in the bicycle came early in the 1960s, when an inventor in England, Alex Moulton, produced a series of machines which had small wheels – 16 inches (approximately 40 centimetres) in diameter as opposed to the normal 26 or 27 inches or continental size 70 centimetres. Their other main feature was a rubber suspension to give a smoother ride.

The smaller wheels meant a more compact bicycle, and he extended the idea by using a frame without a traditional cross-bar, in an F-shape instead of a diamond. The main tube, from steering head to bottom bracket, could on some models be taken apart, so that the machine – or indeed several machines – could be loaded easily into a car boot.

The small wheel without the suspension gave a very rough ride, and other companies trying to imitate the Moulton without the cushioning effect soon settled for a compromise 20 inch (approximately 50 centimetres) wheel, which gave compactness and a modern look.

Several new designs for children's bikes were tried in the 1970s, but by 1980 a really revolutionary cycle design was established which has changed the world of cycling for ever.

The thick, soft
tyres and plastic
'mag' wheels of the
BMX are well suited to
stuntwork.

This was the BMX (bicycle moto-cross) machine. Built for stability and ruggedness, it has a thick-tubed but small, squashed frame, small wide wheels with strong knobbly tyres, hub brakes, wide handle bars bolted to the head tube, and other components adapted from motorcycles.

The BMX made it possible to ride over rough ground and do leaps which would wreck a conventional bike in half an hour. It was also stable enough to do all sorts of low-speed acrobatics.

BMX clubs, racetracks and parks sprang up all over the country, and it wasn't long before grown-ups wanted to share in the fun. They developed a larger

version, known as the mountain bike (or all-terrain bike). This had components that would carry an elephant, a very wide range of gears, thick tyres and wide handlebars. Mountain bike races became the new craze.

Then, in 1984, Alex Moulton produced a new version of his small-wheeled bike with suspension. This had a much lighter frame and derailleur gears, and could be used with a fairing. It was as quick as the fastest racing bikes and as comfortable as the best touring bike.

After almost a hundred years of supremacy, the conventional drop-handlebar, diamond-frame design found serious challengers.

The Moulton AM14
updated Moulton's
previous ideas, and its
performance matched
that of the best
conventional bicycles.

Keeping your wheels off the ground – five excellent reasons for having a BMX.

CHOOSING YOUR BICYCLE

Any motorist would be sure to turn a few heads going shopping down the High Street in a Formula One racing car, and he'd certainly raise a laugh taking a sedate family saloon on to a Grand Prix race track. Neither car is built for the job.

It's the same when it comes to choosing a bicycle. You have to take into account the kind of job you want it to do. Buying the kind of bicycle which isn't designed for your purpose means you won't be satisfied, and you won't enjoy cycling as much as you might on the 'right' machine.

There are many kinds of specialist bicycle, and a specialized bicycle isn't necessarily an expensive bicycle. Look at your local postman's bicycle; it's sturdy and undoubtedly sluggish, but it has plenty of carrying capacity, and has been designed to remain stable even when bearing a full bag of mail.

Enthusiastic cyclists and conscientious cycle dealers all like to see people enjoying cycling, no matter what kind of riding they want to do. And that means not trying to ride a long distance on a bicycle built for local shopping, or expecting a thoroughbred racing machine to bump up and down kerbs without protest.

The term 'push-bike' seems to suggest immediately that cycling is hard work – but if you've the

Study the bicycles available in a good cycle shop before deciding what to buy.

right bicycle for the job, it needn't be.

Sometimes you see young people obviously out on a long tour struggling along with what manufacturers choose to call 'sports' bikes. These have a sporty look, but it's deceptive. Sports bikes usually have the cheapest components, are heavy and badly built. They are all right for riding around town, but load them up with camping gear, set off on a tour, and you'll regret it. Even more so if you haven't taken care to pack only the things you really need, and to invest in a lightweight tent, sleeping bag and so on.

You probably won't look back on that particular tour with pleasure. You may even come back, put the bicycle in the garden shed with a sigh of relief (or worse, in the 'for sale' columns of the local paper), having had your cycling ambitions well and truly blunted.

It could have been different. You might have been riding lightweight machines, and carrying the very minimum of luggage, the tent and sleeping bags in lightweight materials, or the need for a tent simply replaced by the use of youth hostels.

So before you start browsing through catalogues, or wandering down to your local cycle shop, think what you want a bicycle for – what kind of cycling you want it to provide for you.

You'll know, of course, roughly how much you have to spend, and that immediately puts some limits on your choice. But within your budget, do you want a bicycle on which you can race *and* do some pleasure riding? If so, is the gear range right for both uses?

Maybe your ambitions don't extend that far. Perhaps you just want a bicycle for riding locally, with plenty of capacity for carrying – maybe shopping, maybe sports gear, maybe the things you need for school – it needs to be comfortable, and have built-in lighting perhaps; a bicycle built not for speed but for long and steady service.

You can get advice, of course. If you know a regular cyclist, he or she will help. And a reliable cycle dealer won't just be out to make a quick profit by selling any old bicycle to you. He too should be interested in finding the right bicycle for your needs, and making you a satisfied customer – after all, buying a first bicycle is one step towards becoming a lifelong cyclist, and cyclists buy a lot of spares in a lifetime!

Second-hand bicycles

If you can't afford a new bicycle, you may wonder about second-hand 'bargains'. Maybe you know someone who heard of someone else who once bought a 'real racing bike' for next to nothing, or who made up a really good machine from bits and pieces found on rubbish dumps. Maybe, maybe . . .

The trouble is, you need to be a good mechanic to tell whether a second-hand bicycle really is a bargain. A resprayed frame might hide a history of crashes or a nasty attack of galloping rust. Buckled wheels might have been trued so often that the spokes are tighter than bowstrings, and the slightest bump will turn an apparently good round wheel into a figure-of-eight.

So if you're offered a second-hand bicycle, enquire into its

TYPES OF CYCLE

Touring cycle

Racing cycle

Mountain cycle

44

Lady's frame

Mixte frame

Tandem

Small wheeled cycle

Make sure your bicycle 'fits' you

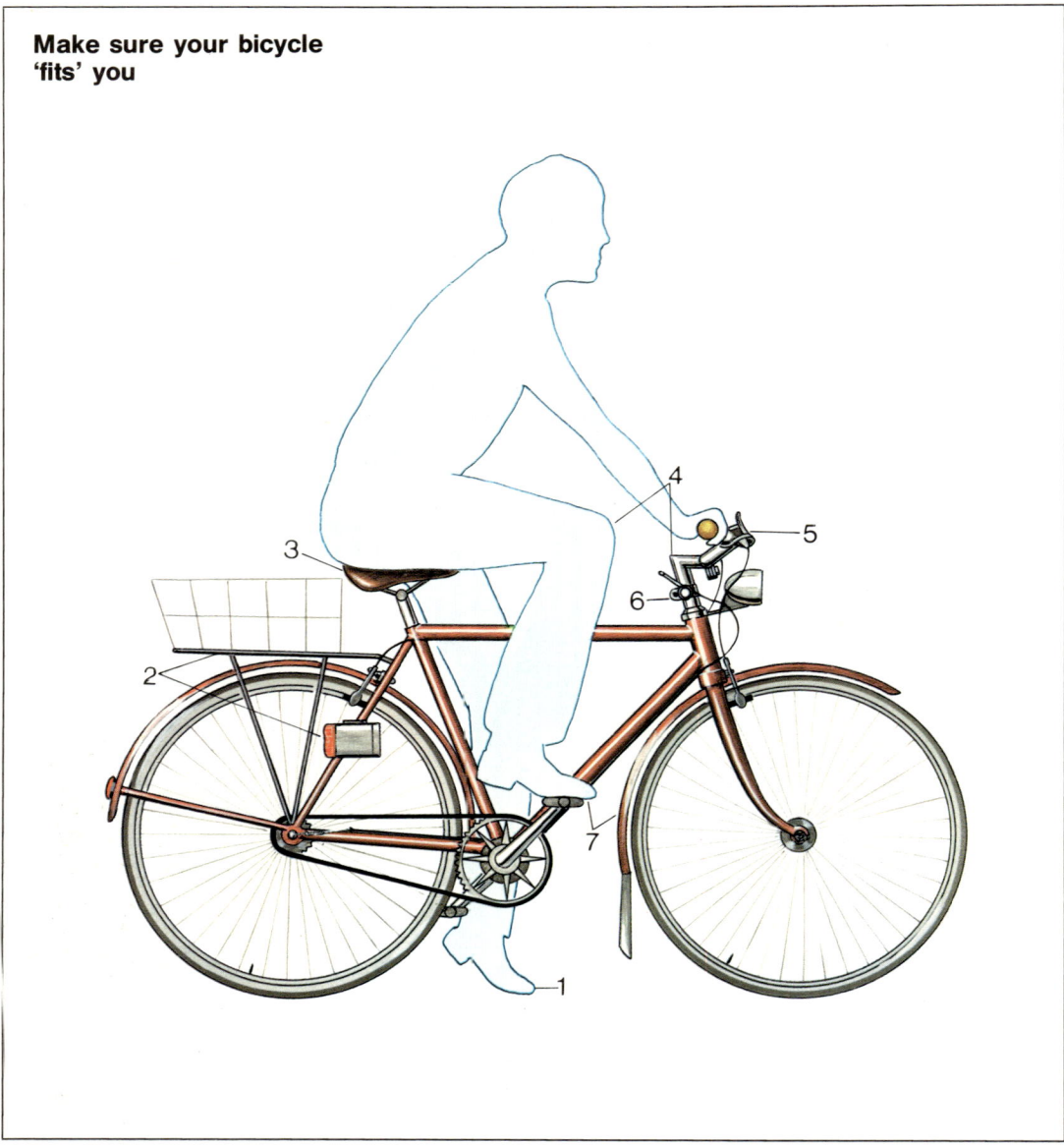

1 Sit on the bicycle with hands on the handlebars. Adjust the saddle so that both toes can reach the ground – or, so that if one foot is on a pedal the ball of the other foot is on the ground.

2 When pedalling, heels shouldn't touch the back carrier or lights.

3 Saddle and handlebars should be approximately level for ordinary day-to-day riding. Before buying a bicycle check that both have enough adjustment to give a comfortable riding position.

4 Knees and body shouldn't touch the handlebars while riding or turning.

5 Brake levers should be easy to reach and should suit the size of your hands.

6 Gear levers should be easy to reach and work.

7 Toes shouldn't hit the front mudguard when the wheel is turned (the ball of the foot should be on the pedal).

As a very rough guide, the bicycle's frame size should be 25 centimetres (10 inches) shorter than your inside leg measurement.

Checking a second-hand bicycle

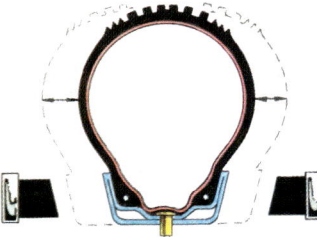

A buckled wheel can be detected by spinning it and watching the brake blocks. The distance between the wheel rim and the block will alter if the wheel is buckled.

Worn tyres, especially where the canvas is starting to show through, must be changed.

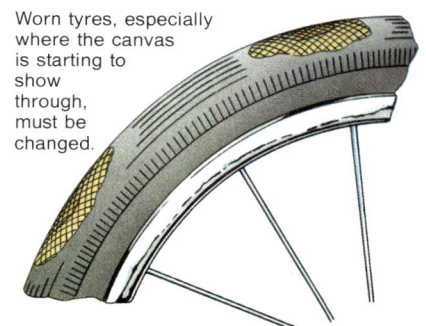

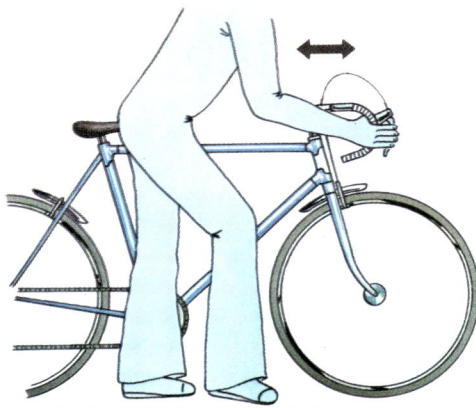

Apply the brakes and 'rock' the bicycle forwards. Any movement in a loose headset will then be felt.

Check rear sprockets and chain wheel teeth. Both can be hooked from wear, and this can cause the chain to jump.

Badly-worn or unevenly-worn brake-blocks should be changed.

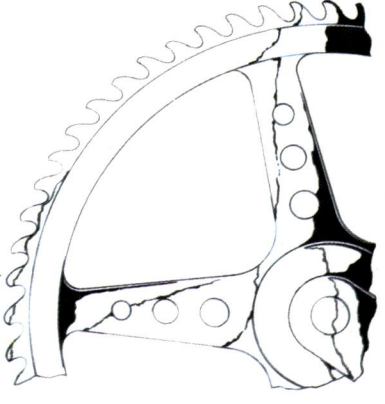

history and hope for a truthful answer. Stay clear of bicycles which look as if they might have been in crashes. Steer well away from front forks which look bent back – even slightly.

If the paintwork is original, then watch for rust. Even if it isn't, you can still detect the roughened patches underneath a re-spray job if you look hard enough. And ask why the re-spray has been done.

Spin the wheels to make sure they run true. Keep your eyes on a fixed point, such as one brake block, and see if the rim of the wheel appears to move closer or further away from the block as it spins. Beware as well of spokes that are so tight they won't 'give' a little.

Test the steering, which should be smooth. You don't want any play in the head bearings either; test this by applying the front brake and then pushing the bicycle forward, against the brake's resistance. If you feel any movement (and you might even hear it as well) then the headset needs tightening. Riding the bicycle and using the front brake with a loose headset will also produce a 'juddering effect'.

Look at the transmission. Having to replace the chainwheel, chain and freewheel because they're very worn is an expensive business. Look closely at the profile of the chainwheel teeth. Are they hooked in profile? If so, then they're dangerously worn.

Expect to replace some items anyway. A second-hand bicycle will usually need new tyres and tubes; it's also worth the comparatively small expense of replacing brake blocks, gears and brake cables. A new chain won't hurt either, but if you replace the chain, then you will almost certainly have to replace the freewheel as well, because the two will have worn down together, and replacing one without the other is bound to mean transmission problems.

If you don't feel happy about checking these points yourself, then ask an experienced cyclist friend. Best of all, buy from a dealer who'll give you a guarantee for your 'new' second-hand bargain, after having serviced the machine himself.

But above all, make sure that the bicycle you choose is right for the kind of cycling you want to do.

Buying a new bicycle

There's as much difference between bicycles in style, purpose and price as there is between a Mini, a tractor and a Grand Prix racing car.

Sophisticated materials have made a top racing bicycle a thing of wonder and beauty – but the cost could make you wince.

Yet now, more than ever, it is possible to choose the right kind of bicycle from ranges of inexpensive machines. Designers and engineers from big manufacturing companies have spent much more time working on models for the average person than they have for the few who will spend a lot of money on the best bicycle that can be produced.

Once you're out of the young children's ranges, bicycles fall into several well-defined categories: out-and-out roadsters, for comfort and long life; shoppers or folders, for convenience; 'sports' bicycles, for the user who wants leisure cycling as well as a means of getting to the shops; and machines specially designed for enthusiasts, be they the keenest of tourists or really dedicated racing cyclists.

The 'fun bike'

In the mid 1970s a new kind of children's machine started to appear in thousands, and there are still plenty around, in use and on sale, although the initial craze has died out.

These are 'fun bikes' modelled on the weird American motorcycles generally called choppers.

Typical features of these machines are 'high-riser' handlebars, which extend not outwards or downwards, but upwards, with the result that your hands are in a much higher position on the bars than they would be with conventional machines.

Because children have the urge to imitate the acrobatics of American stunt riders, and above all to do 'wheelies', lifting the front wheel off the ground while the bicycle is on the move, the designers of fun bikes set the saddle right back over the rear wheel, and gave it a back-rest for safety, while making the front wheel smaller. This, together with the high-riser handlebars, makes a 'wheelie' very easy.

Apart from this, fun bikes are expected to get a lot of hard use, to be ridden over rough ground without breaking up. What they also get – which is stupid and probably illegal, is their riders trying to carry passengers, making use of the long, banana-shaped saddle.

Fun bikes aren't serious cyclists' machines. They can't carry a lot of luggage and they won't go long distances.

▽ The banana bike, a 'fun' version of the recumbent cycle. Lie back and enjoy yourself! The strange projection in the front serves as both a crash protection and a towing bar.

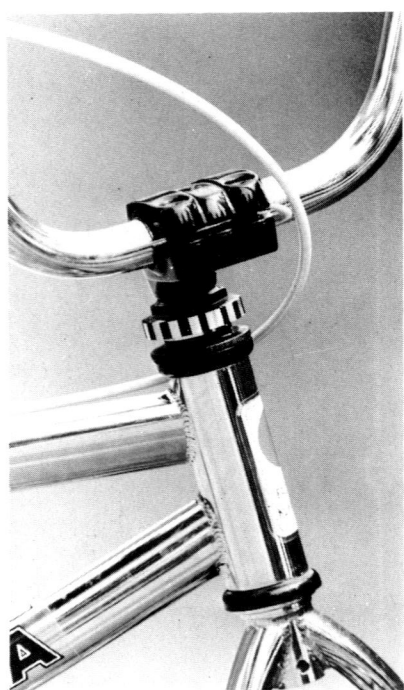

◁ BMX handlebars are clamped firmly into place. The frame is heavily welded and outsize pedals are normally fitted to ensure maximum control in the wildest situations.

The BMX

The BMX is probably the most exciting bike you can buy, so long as you don't want to travel very far on it. It's built for having fun on, not for carrying sackloads of luggage or for long days toiling up mountain passes.

When choosing your BMX, you should decide whether you want it for racing or for stunting. Stunt bikes have stronger wheels, sometimes single pieces of plastic with five hefty spokes, to take the considerable impact of landing from a ten-foot jump. They also have no freewheel, which enables you to pedal backwards, and to keep the bike upright while standing still. Some also have stunt nuts, which are extensions to the wheel hubs on which you can put your feet to perform some of the fancier tricks.

Racing BMXs have a lighter frame made of chromoly, and usually have spoked wheels. You can still jump and do stunts on them, but you should take a bit more care. There is also a range of racing accessories, number plates, transfers, and so on, which you can attach; but be sure not to make the bike so heavy that it slows you down.

If you're getting a BMX, remember that you'll probably be riding it on the roads at some time, even if your main interest is off-street cycling. On the roads, a quite different set of rules apply. Motorists won't be impressed by your wheelies and endos, nor will pedestrians thank you for bumping up onto the pavement. And not many BMXs have light fittings, so make sure that you're home before dark.

▷ You should choose a much smaller BMX frame than for any other kind of bicycle.

The roadster

You have to admire the aristo-cratic lines of the traditional roadster bicycle. It has the style of a vintage car and the comparative comfort of an easy chair.

It isn't a lightweight, and could weigh a hefty 20 kilograms (44 pounds) because of all the sturdy steel parts it uses. Usually en-amelled in a sober dark green, deep blue or black, it is made for comfort rather than speed.

The roadster will usually have 26 inch (approximately 66 centi-metre) diameter wheels. The wheel rims will be strong, and be shod with heavy tyres with prominent tread patterns, to cut down the risk of punctures.

The brakes will be operated by rods working between the brake lever and the stirrups, instead of cables (which are much lighter, but they can break). It will have a sturdy steel frame, steel mud-guards, handlebars and other fittings. Its chainwheel and chain will be enclosed in a case which keeps the clothes away from the oily areas, and the saddle will be well sprung and padded. The treads of the pedals will be made of rubber rather than steel or alloy.

The roadster will have built-in lighting, probably from a Raleigh Dynohub, where the energy for the lights comes from the hub rather than a dynamo generator rubbing on the side of the tyre.

It will usually have gears, and these again will be enclosed in the rear hub, away from dust and dirt thrown up from the road. Hub gears operate quietly, three or four-speed (and sometimes even five), at the click of a switch on the handlebars – all done by meshing cogwheels out of sight of the owner.

For its sheer comfort and reliability this kind of bicycle is a favourite in India and Africa, where the roads aren't always good. And in Holland, where the flat roads lend themselves to cycling, there are few households without one.

The roadster is often modified to become a workhorse. The

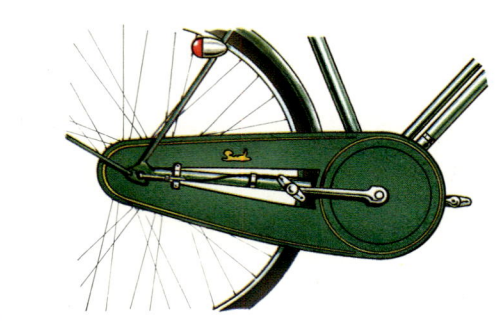

The hub gear and hub dynamo are aids to easy and safe riding.

A roadster

postman's bike is little different in design, although it might lack gears and dynamo lighting. Ice-cream salesmen, delivery boys for butchers and bakers, all use a variant of this bicycle.

One of the problems with a 'normal' bicycle is that you can't carry a lot of luggage. Even a big saddlebag, strapped to the back of the saddle, has its limitations.

You can't safely hang a shopping bag (or anything else for that matter) on the end of a handlebar, nor suspend it from the crossbar. You can get special cycling bags to carry on your back, called musettes or 'bonk-bags', but similarly they too can only carry a limited amount.

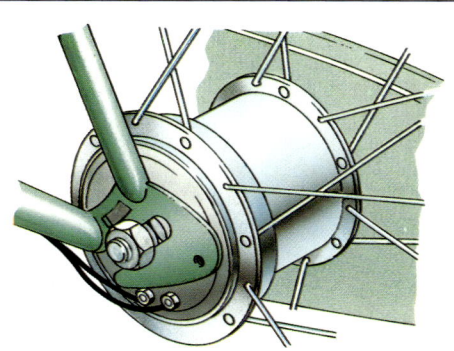

An all-enclosing gearcase keeps the transmission protected from the elements.

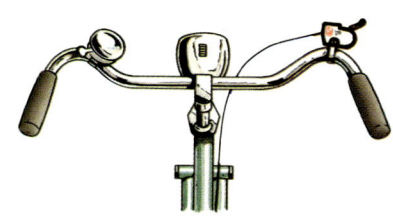

Handlebars are 'sit up and beg', ideal for the utility rider.

This solid, robust roadster might be straight from the factory, or it might be a veteran of the 1920s. Its lines have barely altered for many decades, and it has been adapted for countless purposes throughout the world.

The lady's roadster makes a handy bicycle for city riding.

The bicycle is a popular mode of travel in Africa.

The lady's roadster

When it comes to meeting the needs of women buyers, cycling manufacturers have developed a version of the standard roadster machine which is easier to ride. This range of machines might well be called ladies' tourers (not to be confused with specialized tourist machines mentioned later).

A typical lady's tourer has a smart, bright-coloured finish, with white-wall tyres and cable casing to match.

The frame won't have a cross-bar, so it's much easier to mount and ride if you're wearing a skirt.

The handlebars will be straight, and the brakes will be operated by cables, not rods. Instead of the full chaincase, there will be a lightweight chain-guard, to stop oil from the chain getting on clothes.

Probably there'll be a small saddlebag strapped to the saddle, and to complete the comforts, a three-speed hub gear, built-in dynamo lighting and a comfortable, well-sprung "mattress"-type saddle.

The gear lever for the three-speed has a trigger switch.

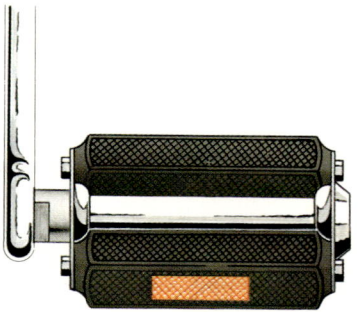

Reflectors on the rubber pedals are a safety aid.

A neat and modern-looking front light for the dynamo.

But otherwise, the components are those of a normal roadster machine, with steel mudguards, sturdy steel wheel rims and other accessories, and a heavy frame built to last.

The lady's tourer (and there are similar models for men) is made for short trips, not long-distance work. Certainly not a speed machine, but one that can be enjoyed for casual riding.

The small-wheeler

The solving of this luggage problem came as a spin-off from the launching of the 16 inch (approximately 40 centimetre) wheeled Moulton machine, which was compact and comfortable. Other manufacturers launched their own small-wheelers and found that without the suspension mechanism of the Moulton, it was a rough ride indeed; so they sought a happy medium, and almost all have settled on 20 inch (approximately 50 centimetre) diameter wheels for their small-wheelers.

Smaller wheels mean you have more luggage room above them before you come to the handlebars or saddle. All small-wheelers are compact, and easy to store as well. Some even fold in the middle to be quickly stowed away in a cupboard or car boot.

▷ The small-wheeler, or shopper, is handy for making short journeys around town, and carries a reasonable amount of luggage. Braking and handling can be uncertain, especially in the wet. Many cycle hire shops offer them, but don't be too ambitious about using one for a long journey.

Those machines where a feature is made of this ability to become a 'beast of burden' are sometimes called 'shoppers'.

They have, fixed to the handlebars, either a removable basket or a rack to which a bag can be fastened. There are similar facilities at the rear. Again, hub gearing and dynamo lighting are frequent features of these machines, which have become a boon to the shopper.

Another advantage of the small-wheelers is that, unlike the usual men's machine, they have no crossbar. The F-shaped frame is more like a conventional women's model, allowing you to 'step through' the frame when you mount, rather than having to swing your leg high over the crossbar. This means one size of machine can fit a whole family. So the small-wheeler has become the 'family bicycle', used by all and sundry. Its compactness means it can be put into a car boot and taken on country excursions, to be used for local exploring by whoever wants to at the time. To adjust the small-wheeler to your size is normally the work of a moment, using quick-release levers at the front and rear to move the handlebars and saddle up or down.

This is the kind of cycle you can frequently hire at pleasure spots or seaside resorts. For the hiring firm, a bicycle which fits almost everyone is clearly a paying proposition.

The small-wheeler does, however, have disadvantages. Most are still rather heavy, and so aren't suitable for travelling long distances. They are for convenience rather than for serious cycling. With their sturdy frames and padded saddles they are right for comfort at low speeds.

A small-wheeler is an ideal 'family' bicycle.

The saddle and the handlebars can be easily adjusted.

So the bicycle can be used by adults and children.

The sports bicycle

Next machine up the line is the sports bicycle. Some manufacturers will call any machine with dropped handlebars and variable gears a 'racing bicycle', when it is far from being a machine right for racing. The sports machine is halfway towards a true racing bicycle, because it uses lighter components and is designed to go faster than the roadster or the small-wheeler.

The frame is lighter for a start. It may be made of a lightweight tubing, cast rather than welded, though probably still held together with rather rigid and heavy lugs, not butted as in the case of more expensive, lighter and more flexible frames.

Design gives the sports bicycle a generally shorter wheelbase than the roadster, with the result that riding feels more lively and steering is lighter.

Most sports machines have dropped handlebars, which give a choice of riding positions: either on the drops, with the back bent nicely for streamlining, or with the hands on the top parts of the handlebars – an easier position which allows a more upright riding style. The brakes should be positioned so that you can reach their levers with your hands in either position.

Just looking at a sports bicycle it seems that comfort is not the first consideration. The saddle is a fiercely-shaped thing in leather or tough plastic, with no sign of springs or padding. In fact this kind of saddle – also used by racing cyclists – is far more comfortable on longer rides than the 'mattress' used on roadsters. It gives support to the bones of your pelvis.

If you are new to this kind of saddle, you might get a touch of 'saddle soreness' at first, but it soon wears off as you become used to your new seat.

The sports bicycle wheels are usually 27 inches (approximately 68 centimetres) in diameter – a dimension which almost, but not quite, matches the 70 centimetre size used in Europe (you may regret this if you need to replace a tyre or wheel when touring in Europe). The tyres are lighter, with valves in the inner tubes which enable them to be pumped to high pressure (HP) – something like 6 kg per square centimetre (90 pounds per square inch), or six times the pressure of the air around us.

Look at the contraption hanging from the rear hub – that's a *derailleur* gear. It replaces the all-enclosed hub gear, and is so called because it de-rails the chain (when you pull or push the gear lever) from one rear sprocket to another of a different size.

This means that attached to the hub, instead of a normal single-speed freewheel with perhaps 16 teeth, is a freewheel block, with between 3 and 7 (5 is most common) sprockets of different sizes, perhaps 14-16-18-22-28, which provides a bottom gear ratio half that of the top gear.

Although the derailleur gear, which has springs to push the chain or pull it from one sprocket to another, is open to the elements, and attracts mud and dust far more easily than the hub gear, it has the advantage of being versatile. Changing individual sprockets on the freewheel block is possible and quite inexpensive. If you live in a flat area you might have a close-ratio block, and change to wider-spaced ratios for cycling in hillier country.

The number of gears offered by the freewheel block can be doubled (or even tripled) by having a double or triple chainwheel in front – and there's a derailleur-type mechanism to change from one to another here too.

Although many sports bicycles have single chainwheels, doubles are becoming more common.

Most sports machines dispense with a dynamo, and leave you to fit battery lights if you wish. Components are lighter, with alloy replacing steel in many cases for wheel rims, handlebars and extensions, and sometimes for chainwheels, cranks and pedals as well.

Most sports pedals are made of steel however, and offer the possibility of fitting toe clips and straps. These allow you to make more use of your leg power by pushing forward and down on the pedals, then pulling them up too. It sounds unsafe to have your feet 'strapped in', but it isn't necessarily so. In practice the straps need not be tight to give the benefit of using them, and they certainly stop your feet from slipping off the pedals.

Your sports bicycle may or may not have mudguards, or it may have a shortened form of mudguard much in vogue but of little real use in the rain. Any mudguards will be of plastics or alloy, not steel.

Lightness starts to be more important with this kind of bicycle, with weights generally down below 14 kilograms (30 pounds).

With a sports bicycle you can ride a fair distance, go touring for weekends or longer, and with a few changes you can race on it. But whatever you want to do on it, it should be a pleasure to ride.

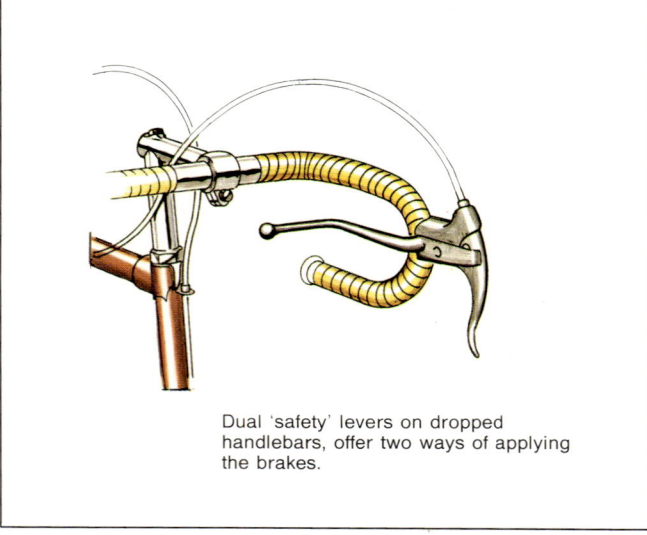

Dual 'safety' levers on dropped handlebars, offer two ways of applying the brakes.

The lighter the machine, the easier it is to pedal. And the more fun you get out of it. So always try out a bicycle before buying it.

A sports bicycle

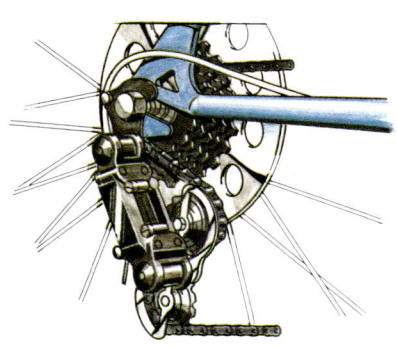

A spoke disc protects against a badly-adjusted derailleur gear sending the chain into the spokes.

Short, fashionable mudguards are often found on sports bicycles – but they are useless in the rain.

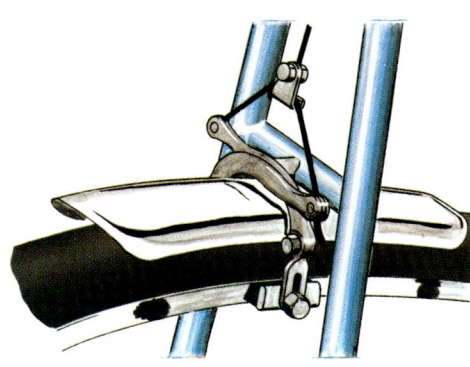

The sports bicycle will probably be your first 'proper' cycle, to use while you decide whether you want to plump for racing, touring or whatever. With up to 15 gears, drop handlebars and narrow-section tyres, it should handle sharply but the fairly cheap steel frame and components will mean that the performance will never match that of a more specialised cycle.

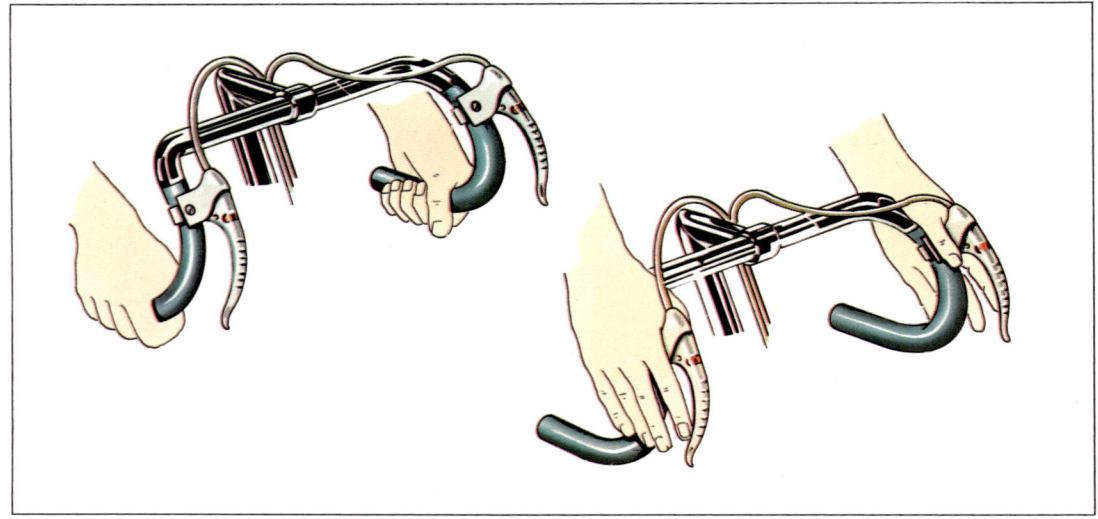

The road racing bicycle

Now let's take a look at a real racing bicycle, although a look may not tell you much, for outwardly a racing bicycle doesn't look very different from the sports machine just described.

It has 27 inch wheels or 70 centimetre in Europe, derailleur gears, a racing saddle, and its design is similar to the sports. But every component will be lighter, using alloy, or even plastics instead of steel wherever possible.

The frame will certainly be of Reynolds or similar tubing (like Columbus or Super Vitus) which is very light yet still strong.

It will have been built with loving care, the tubes joined by carefully cut and filed lugs, or even joined directly with a strong craftsman's weld. If the tubes are not well jointed, then the frame 'whips' from side to side under the stresses of hard pedalling, and some of that pedalling power is lost for ever.

The wheelbase will be shorter than a normal sports machine, and the clearances will not be so great – which means the space between the wheels and the frame will be smaller, because there is no need for mudguards.

Many racing frames will have special fittings brazed on, so that bottle-carrying 'cages', gear

△ Dropped handlebars offer two different hand positions where easy braking is still possible.

A racing bicycle

A cotterless alloy chainset, drilled for lightness – and even the chain has lightweight plates.

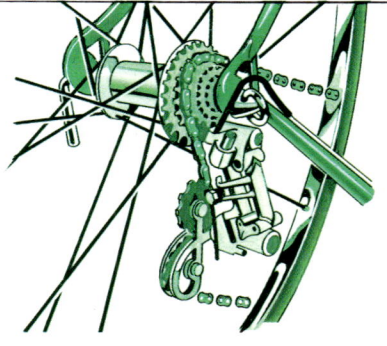

A close ratio freewheel block is ideal for fast courses, where no great differences between gears are needed.

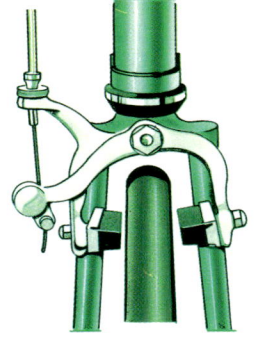

Simple but sophisticated side-pull brake, with a short 'reach' for close-clearance machines.

◁ The racing cycle is the thoroughbred of bicycles: sleek, temperamental and raring to go. Its firm, upright frame means that bumps on the road are transferred straight to the saddle, and every possible ounce has been saved by cutting accessories down to the minimum.

levers and the various gear and brake cables can be attached directly to the frame without having to use screwed-on clips.

Next most important components are the wheels and tyres, and here there are marked differences between the racing and the sports bicycles. The hubs will have quick-release levers, so that the wheel can be removed in a second or two with the flick of a finger, instead of having to work hard with a spanner.

The rims are narrower and are different in design. They are called 'sprint' rims, presumably because they are built for fast work. They don't take ordinary high-pressure tyres, but have special tyres called 'tubulars'. Instead of there being an inner tube, with an outer cover protecting it, and hooked under the outer lips of the rim, the tubular tyre is

a unit. It still has an inner tube, but a much finer one, and the outer cover completely encloses it, wrapped round and stitched underneath, with a tape on top of the stitching to protect it from chafing on the bed of the rim. Because the tubular has no wires, it must be attached in a different way, and is in fact stuck on with special glue, either more or less firm depending on the kind of racing intended. Track racing, because of the strains imposed by the tight bends, needs very firm glue, and usually shellac is used.

The advantage of tubulars is that they can be very light – tyres weighing only 170 grams (six ounces) are not uncommon, but 285 grams (about ten ounces) is a good average – and in the event of a puncture they can be removed and replaced quickly, so that a racing cyclist with a spare tyre

How a derailleur gear works

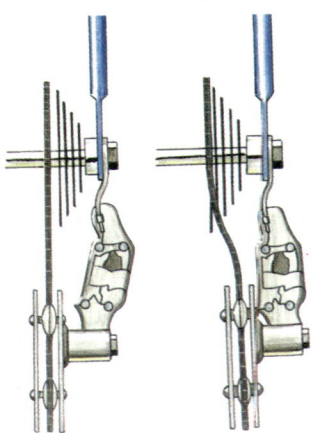

To check alignment, set the chain on the central rear sprocket and see that it lines up centrally *between* the chainwheels. When the gears are arranged with the chain riding on the smallest sprocket and the inner chainwheel, the chain may foul the front derailleur. If it does, turn the adjusting screws until the chain is clear; but does not override the chainwheel.

The derailleur gear works by a strong spring loaded mechanism being compressed or allowed to expand. This movement of the spring, worked by a lever usually situated on the down tube, causes the chain to be literally derailed and carried from one sprocket on the back axle to another. The diagram here shows the chain in the process of being transferred from one sprocket to another.

folded up and strapped under his saddle would lose only a few minutes if he punctured.

There tend to be fewer spokes in a racing wheel. Whereas the roadster might have a 40 spoked wheel, the average racing bike will have 36 spoked wheels, sometimes 28 or even 24. To make a wheel even stronger, the spokes are sometimes tied with fine wire and soldered together where they cross.

Brakes are always of alloy, of either centre-pull or side-pull design, depending on where the cable pulls to activate the brake stirrups. They too can have quick-release levers to open up the distance between the brake blocks to help with wheel removal.

The derailleur gears will use the lightest of alloys. For road racing a six-speed block at the rear and a double chainwheel at the front are common, giving a choice of twelve different gear ratios. With a derailleur gear no time is lost when you change up or down; you must keep pedalling to complete the change, whereas you have to stop pedalling for a hub gear to change.

Usually the twin control levers for the gears are near the top of the down tube, but some riders have them plugged into the ends of the handlebars.

The other main feature is the chainset, which will be of a design which does away with fiddly cotter-pins – the long, tapered bolts which are used to hold steel cranks on their axle, and which quite often work loose.

These cotterless chainsets in alloy have bolts too, but they fix into the squared-off ends of the axle to hold the cranks secure.

For convenience the chainrings of a racing chainset can be easily removed if you want to try a completely different set of gear ratios.

The track racing bicycle

The racing bicycle so far described is for racing on the road, but track racing bikes are far more simple. They have no brakes, no unnecessary projections like quick-release hub levers, and have a single gear with a fixed wheel. This means whenever the rear wheel revolves, so too must the cranks – you can't freewheel but you can use the 'fixed' for slowing down, by exerting a backward force on the pedals. Some expert trackmen can even stand still on the bikes for long periods by using the fixed gear on which to rock imperceptibly back and forth.

You can use a fixed wheel on

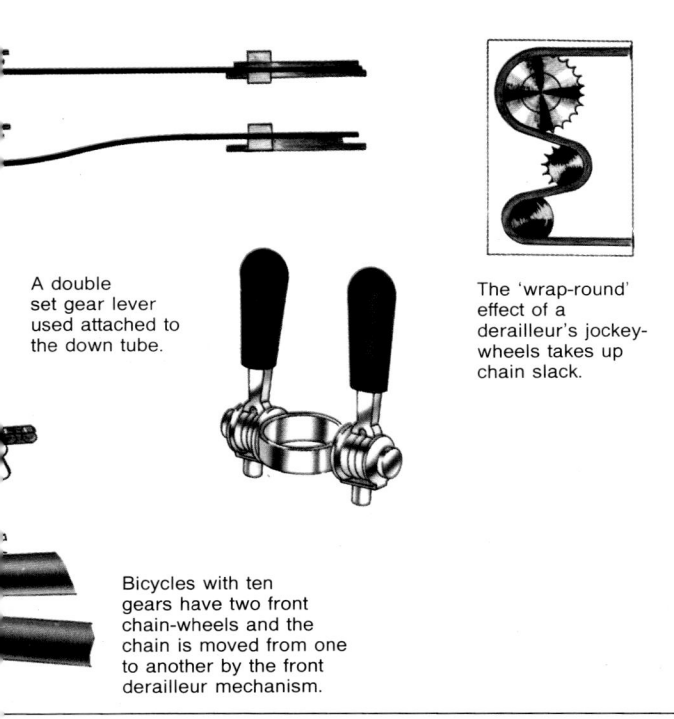

A double set gear lever used attached to the down tube.

The 'wrap-round' effect of a derailleur's jockey-wheels takes up chain slack.

Bicycles with ten gears have two front chain-wheels and the chain is moved from one to another by the front derailleur mechanism.

A four-man track racing team: hard to distinguish between man and machine.

The modern 'low-profile' racing cycle, with cow-horn bars and solid carbon-fibre wheels.

the road, but only for pleasure riding or time trials. It is not allowed in road racing.

In the 1984 Olympic Games, the shape of the track racing bicycle changed dramatically. The United States team introduced the new-style 'low-profile' bike. To cut down air resistance and keep the front as low as possible, the front wheel is smaller than the back. The front tube is much shorter than the seat tube, so that the crossbar is set at an angle, and the usual drop handlebars are replaced with 'cowhorn style bars'. The greatest innovation of all is in the wheels. Again to cut down air resistance on the spokes, the back wheel is solid, with a carbon-fibre disk linking hub with rim. This design performed very well in competition, and is becoming more and more popular for track racing in this country too.

The touring bicycle

Just as the racing cyclist demands a highly specialized machine, so does the enthusiast for touring.

The long distance traveller needs comfort, a bicycle which will travel long distances and over varied terrain, and which will, when required, carry a lot of luggage.

So once again you should aim for lightness, with alloy components wherever they don't bear too heavy a load. The tourist might go for steel rims, for instance, although most are happy to tour on alloy HP rims and tyres.

The frames will be of lightweight tubing but reinforced at the rear triangle (chain stays and seat stays) by the use of a larger-section tube.

Brazed-on fittings could well be similar to those used on racing bicycles, although some enterprising tourists tell their frame-builders to braze on a clip from which is suspended a primus cooking stove!

The chainset will be a double or a triple, with the size of the chainwheels varying enormously, to give an ultra-wide range of gears. For the same reason, the spockets on the freewheel block will have big tooth differences, and this will mean that the tourist may need a special rear gear with plenty of 'wrap-round' movement on its lower arm to take up the slack on the chain.

The tourist will probably have some form of permanent lighting system such as a dynamo set.

The chief feature of the touring machine is, of course, its carrying capacity. Some tourists can travel light, and a large saddlebag will (and can) serve their needs for a fortnight away.

Others want to take their 'house' away with them, planning to sleep under canvas. This means a tent, sleeping bag and cooking apparatus have to be carried somewhere. This is where pannier bags are needed.

Panniers, be they front or rear, are strapped on to pannier carriers either side of a wheel. The carrier, of steel or alloy, is bolted firmly to the machine, usually via the main bolt of the brake and using the mudguard 'eyes' to which the mudguards also bolt. Here again, it is possible to have special fitments brazed on to the frame when it is being built, and many keen tourists do this.

The advantage of pannier bags, carried on a well-fixed pannier frame, is that they don't greatly affect the steering of a bicycle, even when fixed astride

A touring bicycle

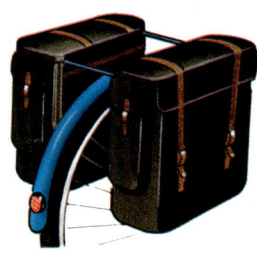

Wide-ratio double chainwheels for use in mountainous areas.

Pannier bags astride the rear wheel — a safe way of carrying luggage.

Centre-pull brakes, a favourite with many tourists.

◁ The touring cycle has a less upright frame than the racer: it is less responsive but much more comfortable. It is also designed to take full mudguards, and panniers on front and back. The best touring cycles can be just as expensive as racers — which is not surprising since they are built to be ridden around the world.

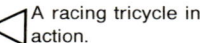
A racing tricycle in action.

This tandem is well loaded for touring

the front wheel, providing that the panniers are well balanced in weight.

The tricycle
There are other types of cycle which have their own enthusiasts. Remember your little tricycle? Well, there are many riders who prefer to ride an adult three-wheeler instead of a conventional bicycle. The steering is strange, cornering a matter of acrobatics, but tricyclists refuse to admit that two wheels are better than three – after all, you don't have to put your foot down when you stop at traffic lights!

The tandem
For those who prefer company when they're riding, there are always tandems, two-seated bicycles where the work is shared and the cruising speed consequently faster – except perhaps uphill, where the extra weight of a tandem is noticeable.

There are tricycles and tandems for touring or racing, just as there are 'normal' bicycles for these two pursuits.

More than one bicycle?

If this chapter makes you start thinking you need more than one bicycle to enjoy cycling, then let me assure you that it isn't so, although many cyclists do have at least two bicycles.

If you buy a good lightweight bicycle and a heavier pair of wheels and a luggage carrier, you can turn that one machine into a touring bicycle or a racing bicycle with the minimum of work. But as your interest in cycling grows, you'll recognize the pleasure and advantage of having bicycles built for one purpose only, riding your 'normal' bicycle for local journeys, another for touring and maybe even a third for racing.

▽ People who ride tandems swear that there's no better way to travel.

RIDING YOUR BICYCLE

Once you've chosen and bought your bicycle, that's one major step taken. After that you must buy any extra equipment necessary, adjust your bicycle to suit your own height and build, and learn how to cycle safely on the road.

Extra equipment

When you've found and bought the right bicycle, there are still some necessary extra expenses. Your bicycle should already have a pump, but if you have to buy one, make sure it fits the tyre valve on your bicycle, as there are three different types of valve.

Lights

If your bicycle doesn't already have lights fitted, then you'll need some, either a dynamo set or battery lamps. Remember, apart from complying with the law and showing a white front lamp and a red rear lamp plus a reflector, during the hours of darkness, you are also doing something towards your own safety.

All sorts of new lights have been brought out recently. Some are brighter, some lighter in weight, some more convenient to slip on and off the bike, some have rechargeable batteries. The prices vary as much as the specifications too, so you'll have to choose what is right for you. But remember that you need your lights all the time in the dark. It's no good having the most expensive battery lamps if the batteries have run out before you get home; on the other hand, dynamo lights tend to go out if the machine is stationary – which can be highly unsatisfactory if you are stopped in the middle of a busy road trying to turn right.

'See and be seen' should be your motto. It's not just a question of lights; make sure you are well equipped with reflectors as well.

New cycles are sold nowadays with reflectors in the spokes, as well as on the rear mudguard. It's a good idea to fit them to your pedals too, if you can, since these catch the attention of motorists very easily. And you should think about the way you are dressed. A light-coloured or orange jacket will be more easily seen than a dark one at any time of day, and in the daylight a fluorescent jacket is very good. For night-time riding, though, you need something that will reflect the cars' headlights, and most people choose yellow reflective belts, which again are very distinctive.

These trans-America riders have made themselves outsize reflectors to warn traffic.

▷ A small mirror attached to the handlebars can be a big help in traffic.

▷ A modern lighting system is slim and gives a bright light.

Security

You will need to buy some kind of lock and chain to secure your bicycle if you leave it for any length of time. You can buy special bicycle locks from your cycle dealer or buy a length of heavy chain and a padlock from an ironmonger.

When you leave your bicycle, chain one of the wheels to the frame and also, whenever possible, put the chain around some-thing immovable like railings or a lamp-post. Take any removable bits and pieces such as the pump and lights with you, and keep a record of the serial number which will be stamped on the frame of your bicycle. If your bicycle is stolen you will need to give the police this serial number.

You can insure your bicycle against theft and accident. Many bicycle shops provide insurance if you buy a new bicycle from them.

Clothing

Dress sensibly for cycling. There are specialized clothes if you intend to become really serious about cycle touring or racing, but you need not spend money unnecessarily if all you intend is gentle pleasure cycling. Just make sure you wear good firm shoes (walking shoes are ideal because they have a strong sole) so that all your leg-power is transmitted to the pedals and not soaked up by the thick rubber sole of a gym-shoe or 'training' shoe.

If you wear long trousers, keep them from being caught by the chain or in the chainwheel by using trouser-clips. Tracksuit bottoms are a good substitute, but the seat is usually worn away quickly by friction on the saddle.

In cold weather, wear a warm jacket or lots of sweaters. Nylon anoraks keep out the wind but make you sweat a lot instead, so only wear them if it's very cold

weather or it starts to rain heavily. And if you do need to ride in the wet, you can buy rainproof jackets or a traditional cycle cape quite cheaply.

The best thing, though undoubtedly the most expensive, is to invest in a jacket made of Gore-tex, a special material that the manufacturers claim is entirely waterproof, but which

◁ Choose equipment carefully. Safety is always the most important factor. Remember to take lights, pump, padlock and wet weather clothing if you are cycling any distance.

◁ A helmet is fairly comfortable to wear, and can save you from serious injury in an accident.

allows your body to 'breathe'. You thus avoid the problem of overheating inside plastic anoraks. Whatever you choose, make sure that the sleeves are long enough to cover your wrists when holding the handlebars, that the shoulders give you room to stretch forward, and that the jacket covers your entire back while riding.

In winter most cyclists like to wear a warm cap: a surprising amount of body heat can be lost through the head. But in recent years helmets have become more popular, particularly for riding in towns. These are made of lightweight plastic, and should protect you from the effects of all but the hardest falls. Some people are reluctant to use helmets, claiming that they are uncomfortable, restricting, sweaty and take away much of the pleasure of cycling. But there is no doubt that they have saved some people from bad accidents; and in racing (especially BMX and mountain-bike racing, where spills are inevitable) they are a necessity.

Accessories

You can buy all sorts of accessories for your bike, some more useful than others. Padded handlebars are undoubtedly more comfortable than the traditional tape, but they can become soggy if the cycle is allowed to stand out in the rain.

New hard-wearing brake blocks are expensive, but give better stopping power in the wet and don't wear out for many miles. Various devices are on sale to save you from punctures. There is a liquid you can spray into your inner tube which will seal the puncture automatically, keeping the tyre inflated for long enough to let you get home; there is also a plastic tape you can put inside your outer tube to stop nails or bits of glass from penetrating through to the inner.

There are all sorts of speedometers and odometers (which count the miles or the kilometres). The simplest work with a counter checking the revolutions of the front wheel, but there are solar-powered electronic models for serious training that tell you anything from overall distance covered to average speed, lap speed, fastest lap, and so on. Prices vary wildly, so make sure that you buy one you really need.

Bells and horns used to be standard features on all bikes, but they are increasingly rare. Most people now rely on shouting (or even whistles, kept at the ready round their necks) to keep pedestrians out of their way.

A mirror is not a bad idea, although you should not rely on it when pulling out to turn right, or into a busy lane of traffic.

A water bottle is definitely worth having with you on a tour or on a long ride.

A good cycling position

There are two considerations when finding a good position on a bicycle: comfort and safety. In practice a comfortable position is also likely to be a safe one, enabling you to keep a good look out for other traffic. But some positions need not take account of road safety, such as the extreme position of a track sprinter, who needs high speed, but thankfully doesn't share a race track with other vehicles.

Adjusting saddles

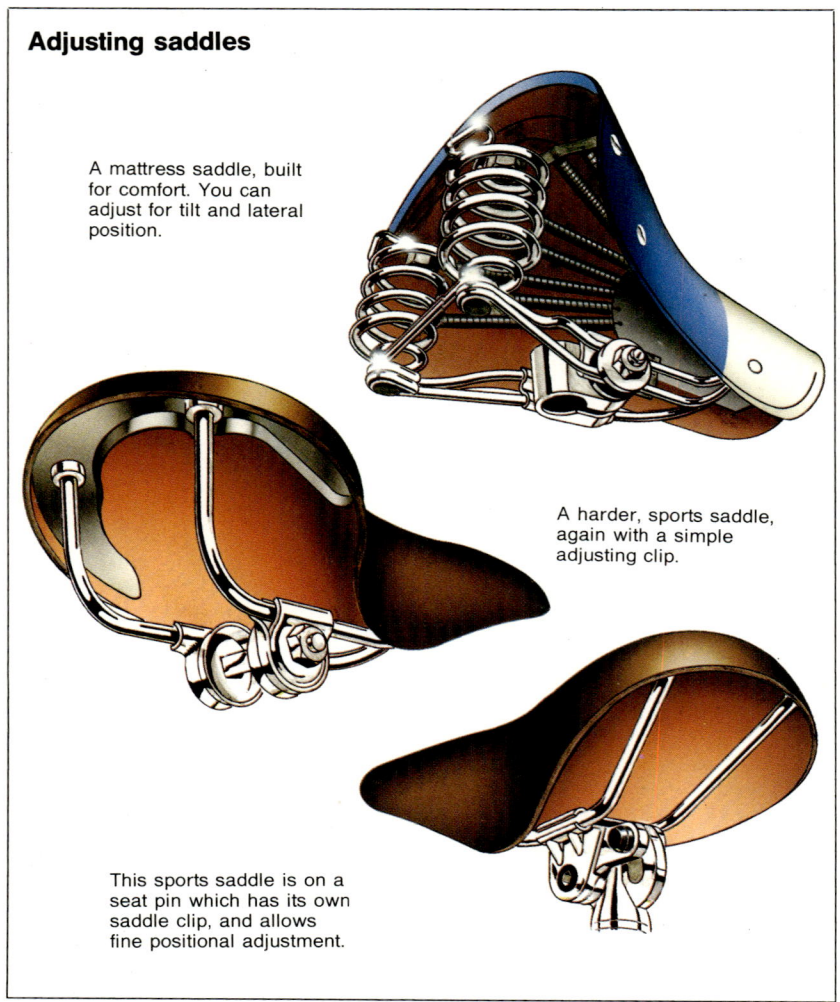

A mattress saddle, built for comfort. You can adjust for tilt and lateral position.

A harder, sports saddle, again with a simple adjusting clip.

This sports saddle is on a seat pin which has its own saddle clip, and allows fine positional adjustment.

Your position on a bicycle should allow you to make the best possible use of your legs to propel the machine, with your body weight distributed between the handlebars and the saddle. Let's first take a look at how to sort out a position for hard road riding, because this is the 'medium' position from which everything else can be assessed.

The most important part of a cyclist is the legs, and so the height of the saddle, plus its position in relation to the bottom bracket, is vital.

Saddle height

Sit on your bicycle. Are you able to touch the floor both sides with the tips of your toes, while still sitting in the saddle? If so, then the bike is probably adjusted about right.

A more exact test is to sit on the saddle, with one heel on a pedal while the crank follows the line of the seat tube; in other words, when the pedal is at its furthest point from the saddle. Your leg should be not quite straight. In this position you should be able to pedal backwards without

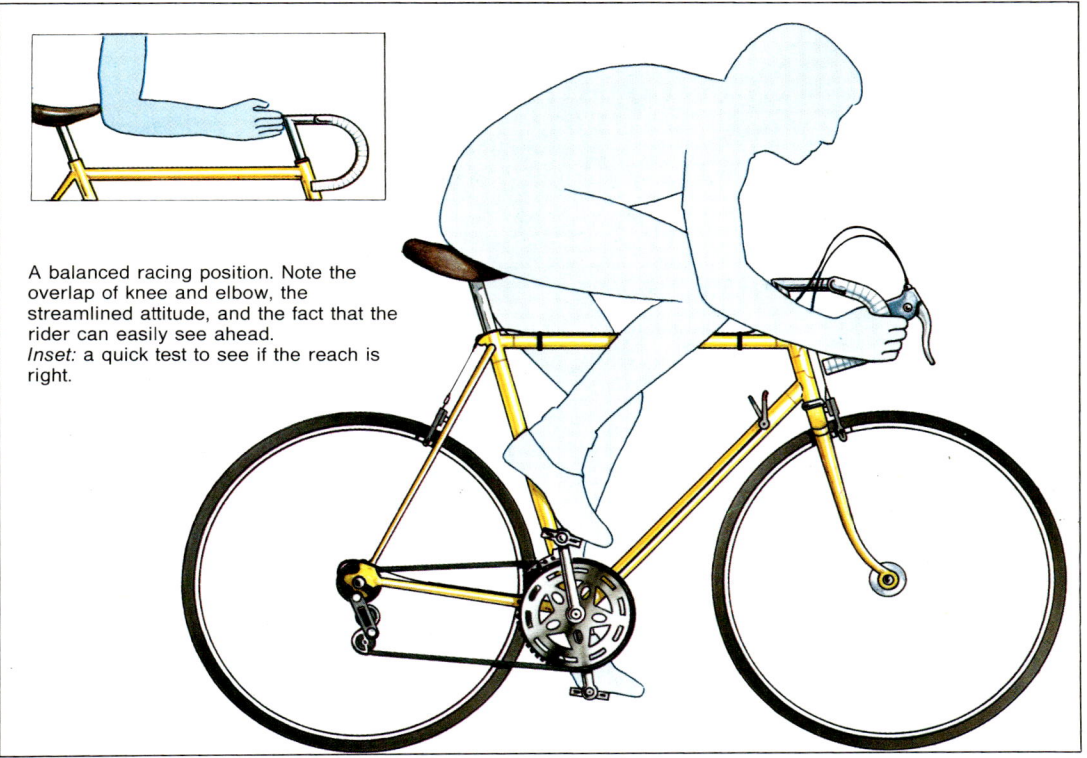

A balanced racing position. Note the overlap of knee and elbow, the streamlined attitude, and the fact that the rider can easily see ahead.
Inset: a quick test to see if the reach is right.

shifting from one side of the saddle to the other.

That's set your saddle height, but a saddle can slide backwards and forwards on its cradle too, and this affects pedalling position. So set your cranks at a horizontal position, with your foot in the pedalling position (use the widest part of the foot over the pedal axle, not the instep). If your saddle position is correct, then an imaginary line down from your kneecap should pass just ahead of the centre of the pedal axle.

As the saddle moves backwards as you increase your saddle height, you'll need to juggle with the two measurements until you get both right.

Also, make sure the top of your saddle is horizontal and never tilted up or down.

Adjusting the handlebars

Now let's move on to the handlebars, the stem and its extension.

The 'rule of thumb' is that with your elbow at the front of the saddle, your outstretched fingers should just touch the handlebars or the tops of your bars if you're using dropped handlebars.

If they fall short, then you need a shorter extension. If they overlap the bars, then you need a longer extension.

The tops of the handlebars should be very slightly lower than the top of the saddle.

In effect, these guidelines should give a position where your knees slightly overlap your elbows at the top of each pedal stroke and your arms are slightly bent when you ride down 'on the drops'.

For good pedalling the broadest part of the foot should be over the pedal axle. Note the way that the ankle comes into play to claw the pedal round on the downstroke. This is called 'ankling'.

This is a road racing position, a happy medium between a leisure riding position, where the handlebars could be raised to be level with the saddle, and a track sprinting position, where the saddle is slightly higher than for road racing, and the handlebars lower. The track sprinting position allows the rider to use his arms and back muscles to a greater degree, but is uncomfortable over long distance.

Remember always that the saddle height is the key to good pedalling, and that the handlebars and stem should be altered to give the right degree of comfort. As well as extensions of different lengths, the other means of altering your position at the 'front end' is to choose handlebars which have shallower or deeper drops, with a greater or lesser forward 'throw'. Remember too that your handlebars should be roughly as wide as your shoulders: if they're too narrow you will feel cramped.

Safety

If you want to use your bicycle to the full, you will have to learn how to ride safely in heavy traffic and on busy roads. Many schools in Britain have visits from police and road safety officers, when the new cyclist can get to know the basics of keeping his or her machine in good condition, and of using it safely on today's roads. And in Britain you can enrol for and take the National Cycling Proficiency Test.

It is very important to learn the basics of road safety.

Basic rules for safe cycling

1 Before starting off from the kerb always look round and make sure the road is clear.

2 Always ride on a cycle path if there is one; if not ride as close to the kerb as you can. Never ride on the pavement. Remember to look out for potholes and any other obstacles that might make you swerve.

3 Obey the rules of the road. Don't ride the wrong way down a one-way street, and don't ride through red traffic lights – car drivers won't be expecting you to do it.

4 Always make sure that you can be seen in the dark. Fit good lights to front and rear, keep the batteries well charged, put reflectors on your wheels, mudguards and pedals and wear light clothes, preferably with fluorescent and reflective strips on them. It's no good riding safely if other road users don't know that you're there.

5 Remember that cars are bigger than you, and that car drivers often say they can't see cyclists; so beware of what they might do. In particular, watch out for car doors opening (especially if you are sneaking down the inside of a row of cars stopped at lights or in a jam), and for cars overtaking you and then turning left straight across your path.

6 Before turning right or left, or moving out to pass stationary or slow-moving vehicles, always look behind to make sure it is safe and give clear arm signals well before you alter your direction in any way.

7 Ride in single file on busy roads and never ride more than two abreast. Remember you must not ride on footpaths or pavements. If there is a safe cycle path along your route – use it!

8 Always keep both hands on the handlebars (unless signalling) and both feet on the pedals. Never hold onto another vehicle or cyclist, and if you are carrying anything make sure it won't tip you off balance or become entangled in the wheels or chain. Do not carry a 'passenger' unless the bicycle is designed to carry more than one person.

9 Remember that your brakes will take much longer to work if it is raining or the road is wet. In these conditions apply the brakes lightly and frequently to wipe the water off the brake shoes and wheel rims, and allow for a much greater stopping distance.

10 Use your common sense – if you are not sure how to cross a busy junction or turn across a stream of traffic, get off and walk.

If you can see where you are going, and other traffic can also see you, then you are likely to be riding safely. Remember that, and you won't go far wrong. Learn and obey the rules of the road which apply in your country. In Britain the Highway Code will tell you everything necessary for good road usage – and in the new (1987) edition there are special sections relating to the cyclist.

Traffic signs

Signs giving orders
These signs are mostly circular and those with red circles are mostly prohibitive.

No entry for vehicular traffic

No right turn

No left turn

No U turns

No cycling

No pedestrians

Signs with blue circles but no red border are mostly compulsory.

Ahead only

Turn left ahead (right if symbol reversed)

Turn left (right if symbol reversed)

Keep left (right if symbol reversed)

Vehicles may pass either side to reach same destination

Route to be used by pedal cyclists only

Mini-roundabout (roundabout circulation – give way to vehicles from the immediate right)

One-way traffic

Warning signs
Mostly triangular.

Cross roads

Roundabout

T junction

Staggered junction

Side road

Bend to right (or left if symbol reversed)

Double bend first to left (may be reversed)

Slippery road

Two-way traffic straight ahead

Road narrows on right (left if symbol reversed)

Steep hill downwards

Steep hill upwards

Gradients may be shown as a ratio i.e. 20% = 1:5

Uneven road

Traffic signals

Pedestrian crossing

Road works

Level crossing with barrier or gate ahead

Level crossing without barrier or gate ahead

Accident drill

If you are unlucky enough to have an accident while out cycling, or be a witness to an accident involving other people – try to remember the following points:

1 Avoid a second collision. If at all possible get yourself (and/or any other casualties) and your bicycle out of the road. If this isn't possible, warn other traffic or ask someone to do this.

2 Do *not* try to move anyone who appears seriously injured. Get help as quickly as possible by going to the nearest house or phone box and calling the police.

3 It is best to disturb an accident victim as little as possible, but if there is a large cut and fast bleeding, press the cleanest piece of cloth you can find firmly over the wound. Hold it tight and try to raise the injured limb unless you think it may be broken.

4 If anyone you are with is hurt, don't panic. Try to reassure them and keep them warm. It is useful to go on a short first aid course if

ever the opportunity arises, but the most important thing after an accident is to get help quickly.

5 If you are going out cycling alone along country lanes remember to tell someone what time to expect you back and give them some idea of your likely route.

6 If you do come off your bicycle remember that even if you are unhurt the bicycle may be damaged. Check it carefully before continuing on your way.

7 If you're unlucky enough to have an accident involving a car, try to get the car's registration number, and the driver's name and address.

Don't let the fear of accidents put you off cycling, but on the other hand try to be as careful and safety-conscious as you can.

M_AINTENANCE_

Now let's look at keeping your bicycle in good condition, for the more care you spend in keeping it clean and well maintained at home, the fewer repair bills you'll have at your cycle shop, and the longer life your machine will have. Maintenance is important for safety too.

Cleaning

A well-enamelled frame will need only the occasional wipe down with a clean rag to keep it clean. But the rest of the machine, especially the steel and chromed parts, need much more attention.

If you can give your bicycle a wipe down after every outing, then you'll never face the major chore of cleaning a bicycle from top to bottom, having to winkle out grime and oily dirt from difficult places, to polish every spoke, and to work on the rust patches on steel parts.

If you can clean it once a week, then you'll avoid the worst of the work. Soapy water gets rid of most of the dust and mud, then metal polish and chrome cleaner will do the rest.

As you become proficient at cleaning bicycles, you'll realize one of the worst problems is that the oil and grease necessary to lubricate many moving parts also attract dust and dirt. So when it comes to lubrication, use just sufficient – any excess oil or grease increases your cleaning problems.

Lubrication

What about lubrication? One fairly recent introduction has

◁ Make cleaning your bicycle a regular job, and it will never be a big task.

▷ Truing the wheels
is a specialist job:
if they are more than
slightly out of line, take
them to a bike shop to
be fixed.

Basic Tool Kit

Puncture outfit
Small adjustable spanner
'Dumbell' spanner
Screwdriver
Allen keys (if your machine has
any allen key fittings)
Tyre levers
Pliers
*Choosing your spanners is a
matter of common sense.
There are several inexpensive
multi-purpose spanners which
use either British or metric
sizes. Pick whichever one
suits most of the nuts on your
bicycle, and let the adjustable
take care of the rest. Similarly,
use a medium-sized
screwdriver, with a blade thin
enough to engage the small
screw-heads on, say, your
derailleur gear adjusters, yet
wide enough to tackle the
bigger jobs.*

Things to Add
Chain-link rivet-extractor
Spoke key

Large adjustable wrench (useful
for headsets)
Phillips screwdriver (if you have
any such screws)
Cable cutter

Once you start building up a
toolbox, it's quite easy to go on
and on, and you'll find yourself
building up a stock of useful
spares, such as gear and brake
cables, spokes and cable casing.
It's always worth having an extra
toe-strap or two as well. They
come in useful for all kinds of
purposes, such as holding your
cape underneath your saddle,
keeping a chain taut if you've
removed the rear wheel (strap it
to the brake-ridge between the
seat stays), or fixing luggage
securely to front or rear carriers.
Satisfy yourself that you have
the tools to tackle any normal
repair job on your bike, and keep
them together in an orderly way.
And don't forget you'll also need
oil or petroleum distillate spray,
plus medium weight grease.

been a great help. Instead of using oil, you can substitute a petroleum distillate spray, which lubricates, throws off water, and is clean – it doesn't attract dirt and grit. Use it on chains, moving parts of derailleur gears, brakes, freewheels – in fact anywhere where you would normally use oil instead of grease.

Pay particular attention to your chain. Before you use a new bicycle, wipe off the manufacturer's grease and start your lubrication from scratch, using the spray or a medium oil, link by link.

Too much lubrication, and dirt is attracted, leaving gooey deposits on the freewheel sprockets and derailleur gear jockey wheels. Too little lubrication, and the chain will develop 'stiff' links, not running smoothly and 'jumping' under pressure.

Lubricate cables with oil or petroleum distillate spray. Most moving parts will also appreciate it wherever there is friction.

The exceptions are places where there are ball bearings, such as the bottom bracket, hubs, pedal spindles, and headsets. These need packing with grease – oil them and the existing grease is only diluted and made less effective. This grease is available from cycle shops.

Happily, even if you use your bicycle very frequently, the bearings need cleaning and regreasing only two or three times a year, and this can be done by a cycle shop mechanic if you don't want to do it yourself. If you can get a chance to watch an expert, then take it. It's fun to find out about how various parts of your bicycle work, and then to maintain them yourself.

Some top-quality parts, such as

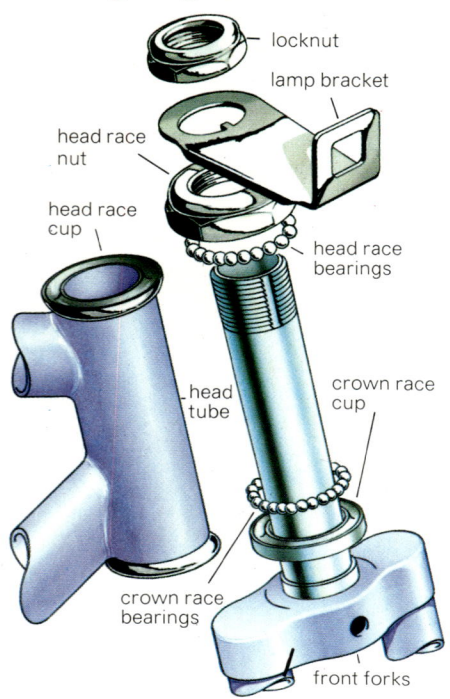

Bearings to grease

locknut
lamp bracket
head race nut
head race cup
head race bearings
head tube
crown race cup
crown race bearings
front forks

Headset ball races need regreasing once a year. Dismantle as shown, line the bottom cup of the crown race with grease, insert the bearings and re-assemble the fork into the head tube. Similarly line the head race cup with grease, insert the bearings and tighten down the head race nut. Adjust by slackening off the head race nut slightly until there is free but not excessive movement. Then fit the lamp bracket and tighten down the locknut.

hubs, pedals and bottom brackets, have sealed bearings which contain enough lubrication for life – so a lot of work is saved if you have enough money to buy them in the first place.

Small repair jobs

Apart from cleaning, oiling and greasing, there are other small jobs which have to be done from time to time.

Until you know a lot about bicycle mechanics, shy away

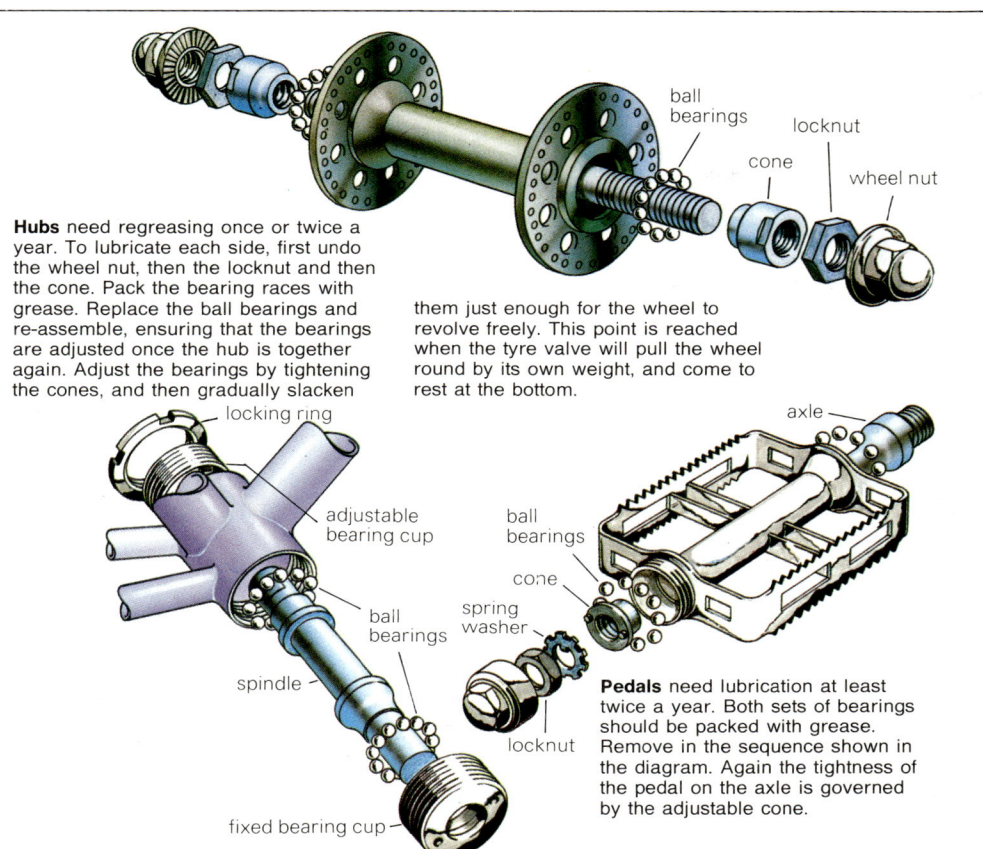

Hubs need regreasing once or twice a year. To lubricate each side, first undo the wheel nut, then the locknut and then the cone. Pack the bearing races with grease. Replace the ball bearings and re-assemble, ensuring that the bearings are adjusted once the hub is together again. Adjust the bearings by tightening the cones, and then gradually slacken them just enough for the wheel to revolve freely. This point is reached when the tyre valve will pull the wheel round by its own weight, and come to rest at the bottom.

Pedals need lubrication at least twice a year. Both sets of bearings should be packed with grease. Remove in the sequence shown in the diagram. Again the tightness of the pedal on the axle is governed by the adjustable cone.

Bottom bracket lubrication is a once a year job. Use plenty of grease, but never any oil. Remove the pedals and chain gear, and then the locking ring and adjustable bearing cup. The adjustable bearing cup unscrews anti-clockwise (the fixed bearing cup – which does not have to be removed for lubrication – unscrews clockwise). Clean, repack with grease, and replace ball bearings. Tighten adjustable bearing cup until there is free movement on the spindle, but no play. Tighten up locknut and re-assemble pedals and chain gear.

from jobs like taking apart freewheels, hub gears and bottom brackets. You'll also need special tools to look after a headset properly. All the other bits and pieces you can happily tackle yourself, learning as you go along how they work.

Gears and brakes
Cables – on gears and brakes – will always stretch as they wear in, so the slack needs to be taken up, otherwise your gear-changing will be very sloppy and your brake levers will have to be pulled a long way before the brakes engage and that's not safe.

Tightening cables is just a matter of slackening a nut on the gear mechanism or brake stirrup, pulling the cable tight with pliers, and tightening up the nut again.

As brake blocks wear down, you need to adjust the brake stirrups to bring the brake shoes containing the blocks closer to the rim. All brakes have an adjusting screw for doing this, either just above the brake lever or just above the brake stirrup.

Derailleur gears need adjust-

Adjusting brakes

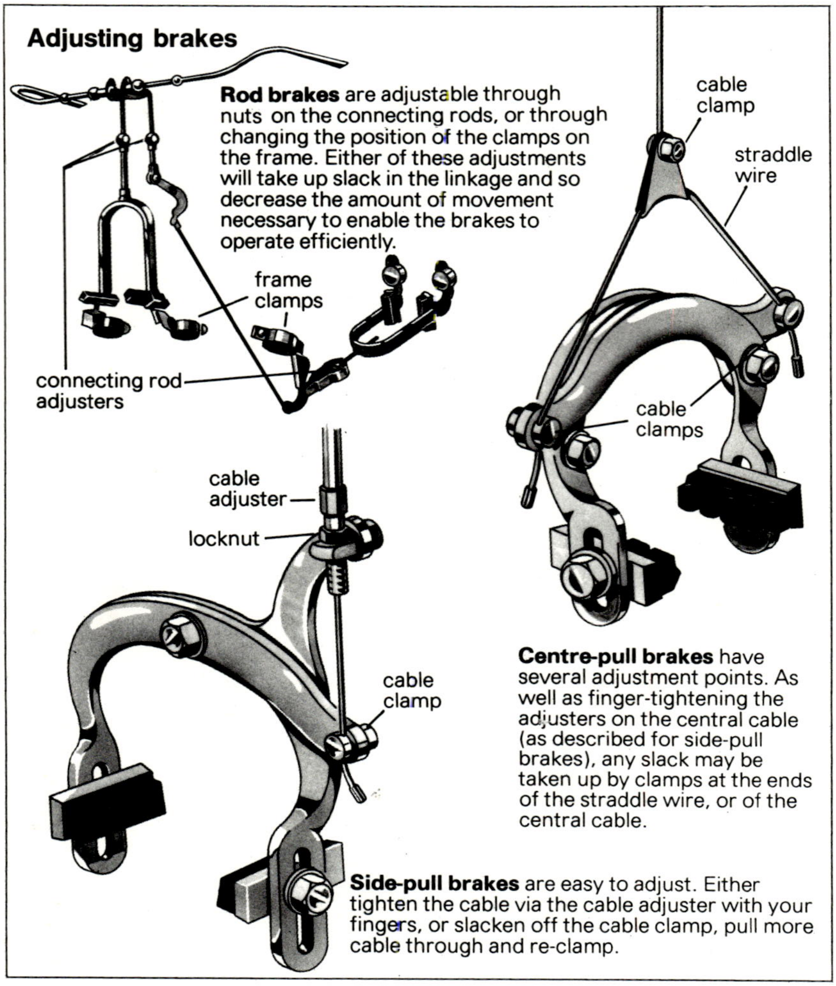

Rod brakes are adjustable through nuts on the connecting rods, or through changing the position of the clamps on the frame. Either of these adjustments will take up slack in the linkage and so decrease the amount of movement necessary to enable the brakes to operate efficiently.

frame clamps

connecting rod adjusters

cable clamp

straddle wire

cable clamps

cable adjuster

locknut

cable clamp

Centre-pull brakes have several adjustment points. As well as finger-tightening the adjusters on the central cable (as described for side-pull brakes), any slack may be taken up by clamps at the ends of the straddle wire, or of the central cable.

Side-pull brakes are easy to adjust. Either tighten the cable via the cable adjuster with your fingers, or slacken off the cable clamp, pull more cable through and re-clamp.

ment too. One recurring job is that if the spring in the gear is too strong for the pressure on the cable at the gear lever, the gear lever will move forward of its own accord. The remedy is simply tightening the bolt on the gear lever itself, thus making the grip on the cable tighter.

Sometimes a rear or front derailleur gear has too much sideways play. The rear gear allows the chain to move into the spokes, or beyond the smallest sprocket. The front changer allows the chain to drop between the small chainwheel and the frame, or at the other extreme, the chain to drop off the outside chainwheel on to the crank. Again, there are screws which adjust this sideways movement in a matter of seconds.

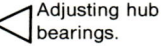

Adjusting hub bearings.

Adjusting gears and headset

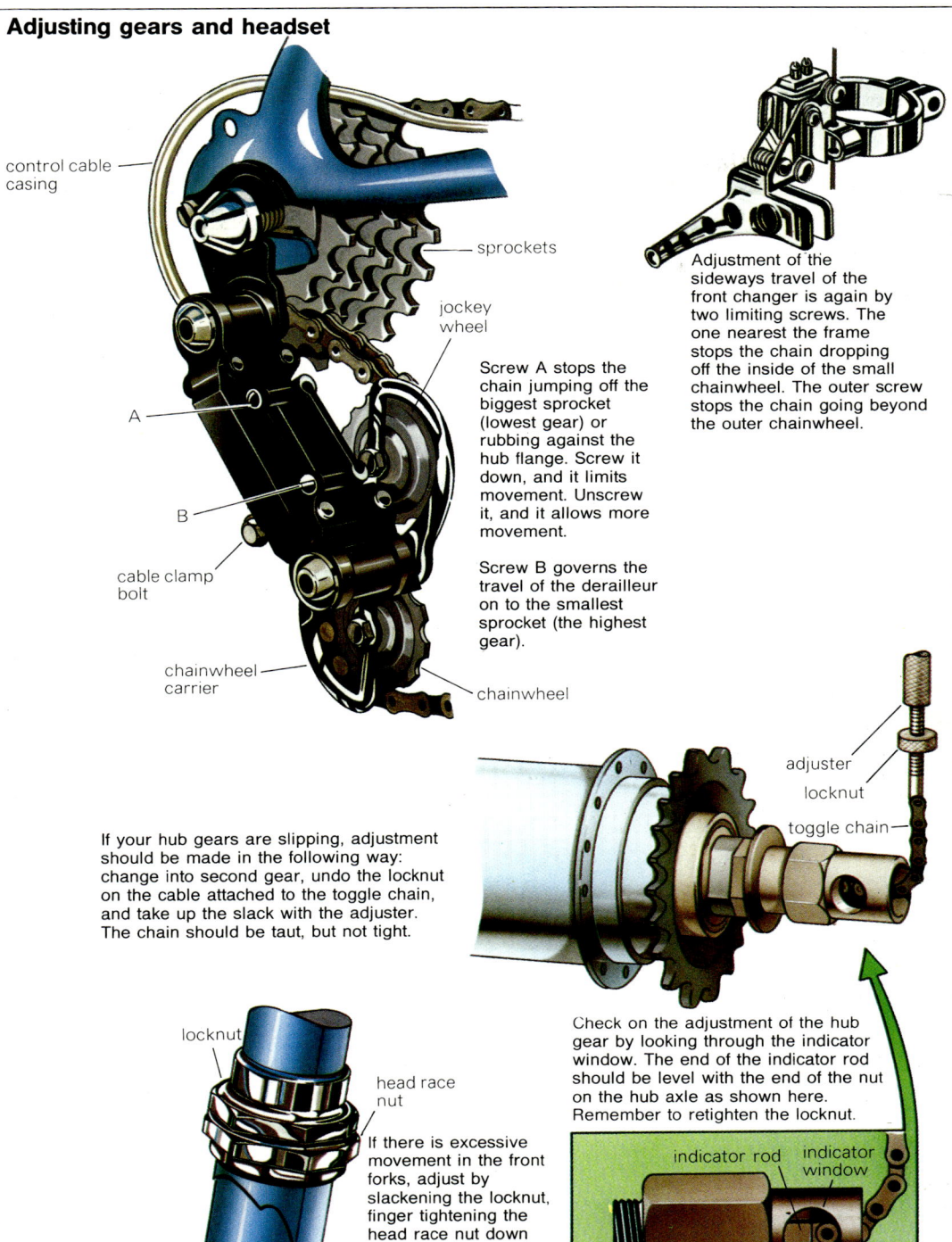

control cable casing

sprockets

jockey wheel

A

B

cable clamp bolt

chainwheel carrier

chainwheel

Adjustment of the sideways travel of the front changer is again by two limiting screws. The one nearest the frame stops the chain dropping off the inside of the small chainwheel. The outer screw stops the chain going beyond the outer chainwheel.

Screw A stops the chain jumping off the biggest sprocket (lowest gear) or rubbing against the hub flange. Screw it down, and it limits movement. Unscrew it, and it allows more movement.

Screw B governs the travel of the derailleur on to the smallest sprocket (the highest gear).

adjuster

locknut

toggle chain

If your hub gears are slipping, adjustment should be made in the following way: change into second gear, undo the locknut on the cable attached to the toggle chain, and take up the slack with the adjuster. The chain should be taut, but not tight.

locknut

head race nut

If there is excessive movement in the front forks, adjust by slackening the locknut, finger tightening the head race nut down on its bearings, and then easing off slightly. Tighten the locknut and re-test.

Check on the adjustment of the hub gear by looking through the indicator window. The end of the indicator rod should be level with the end of the nut on the hub axle as shown here. Remember to retighten the locknut.

indicator rod

indicator window

end of hub axle

Chain maintenance

A standard chain (not used for derailleur gears) is joined by a master or 'spring' link. This spring is easily removed with a thin pair of pliers. It can be prised off, by pushing it with the pliers as shown, and replaced when the chain has been adjusted. The chain can be rejoined by putting the spring link back together in the sequence shown above.

If you need to unrivet a chain, you can take a punch to it, but the best way is to use a link extractor (which can also be used to re-rivet afterwards). Problems arise though, if you force any rivet out completely. Better to use the extractor to push the rivet almost out, then complete the job with the aid of a thin screwdriver. The link is freed with the pivot still engaging the outer plate.

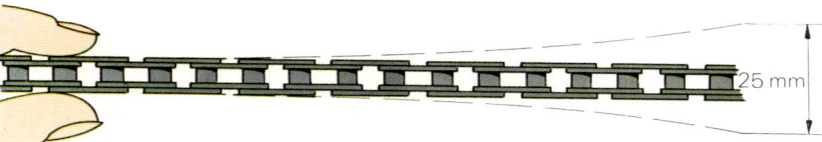

25 mm

Check for too much lateral play. Over about 12 centimetres (5 inches) of chain, there should be no more than 25 millimetres (1 inch) of play.

The headset

If you have a job to turn the handlebars, or if you find the front forks juddering when you use the front brake, then your headset needs to be adjusted, looser for one, tighter for the other.

Slacken off the top locking nut of the headset (at the top of the head tube). Then either tighten or loosen the threaded top ball race with your fingers, making sure that it isn't quite tight down on the ball bearings; retighten the locknut and the headset movement should feel smooth, not too tight and not too loose. If the

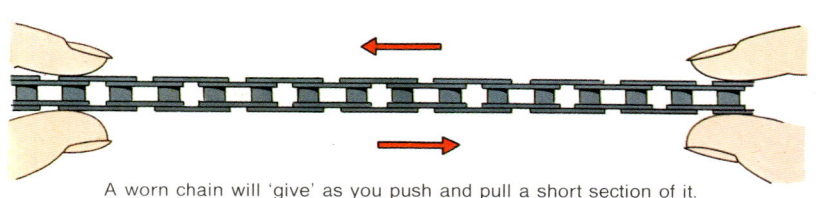

A worn chain will 'give' as you push and pull a short section of it.

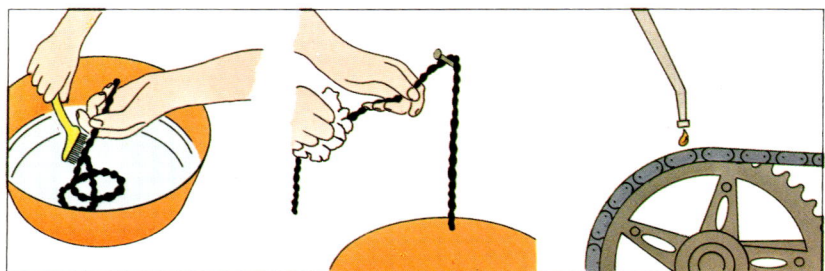

Chains are best cleaned off the bicycle, every 3 months or so. Wipe off as much dirt as possible, then soak in a bath of solvent – e.g. paraffin. Dry the chain thoroughly. Use a little oil or petroleum distillate to lubricate.

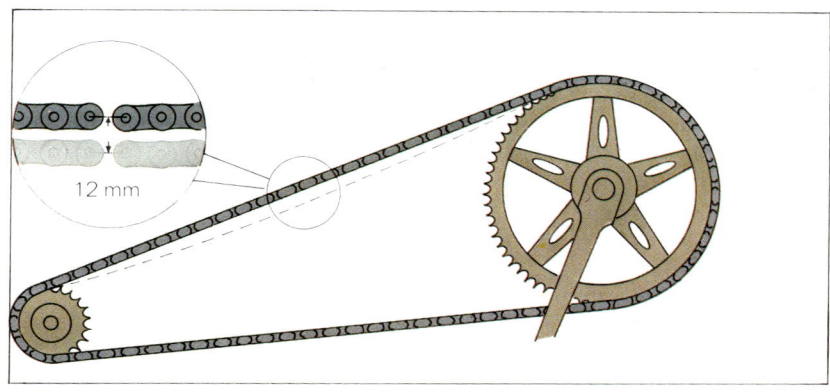

Chains on bicycles without derailleur gears should be quite tight. The amount of play midway between the sprocket and the chainwheel should be about 12 millimetre ($\frac{1}{2}$ inch). The inset shows the amount of movement allowed. Derailleurs take up chain slack automatically.

movement is ever jerky, then one of your ball races is probably pitted, and will have to be replaced – almost certainly a job for the bicycle shop. If in doubt always get professional advice.

Wheel axles
At each wheel axle two cones, one on each side, hold the ball bearings against the bearing surface of the hub. If they are too tight, then your wheel doesn't turn easily. Too loose, and the wheel can be moved from side to side. You'll need two thin spanners (cone spanners) to make this adjustment.

Punctures

You can follow the instructions on your puncture repair outfit which you buy from any cycle shop, but here are the main points to remember when repairing a normal tyre.

1 Use tyre levers to get the outer cover free but don't pinch the inner tube.

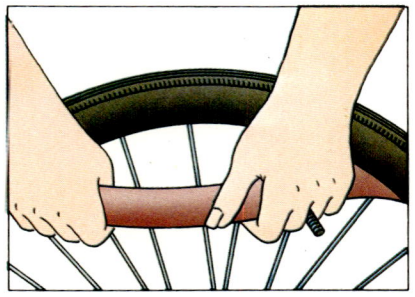

2 Remove the section of the tube where the puncture is, and try to find the cause.

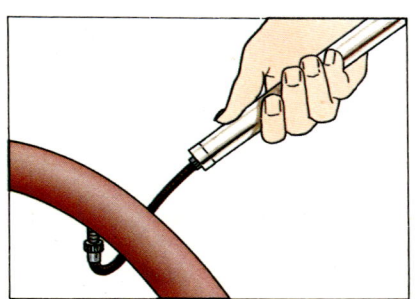

3 If you can't find the puncture site, remove the tube completely and inflate it.

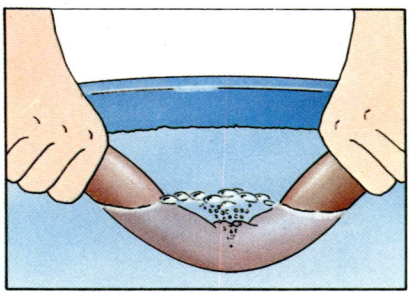

4 Then immerse the tube in water – escaping bubbles will soon locate the trouble spot.

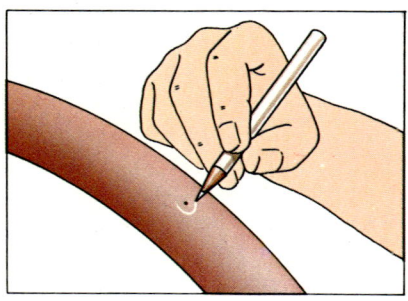

5 Once you've found the puncture, mark the spot with an indelible pencil or biro.

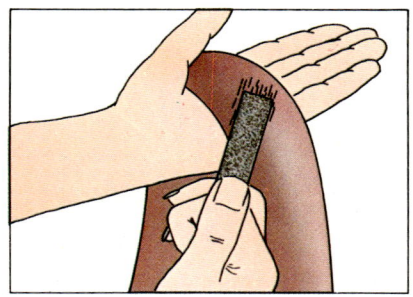

6 Dry the area of the puncture, and roughen it with a fine abrasive paper.

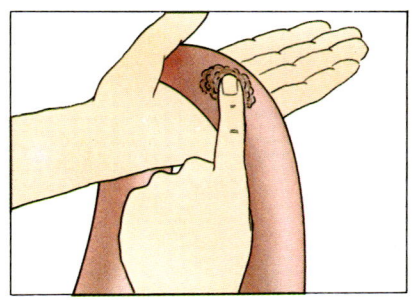

7 Spread rubber solution on the tube and wait for it to become 'tacky'.

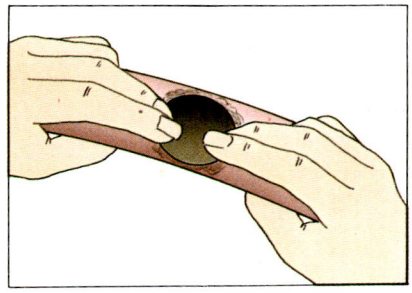

8 Apply the patch and hold it there firmly for a minute or two.

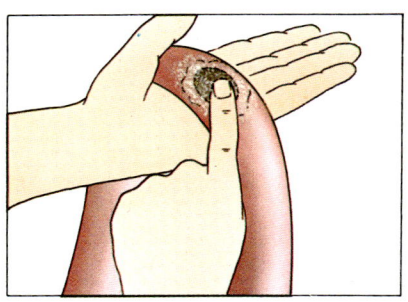

9 Dust the patched area with chalk to remove any stickiness. Slightly inflate the tube.

10 Push the tube back inside the cover and replace the cover. Try not to use tyre levers. Make sure the tube isn't going to get pinched, take a firm grip and roll the cover back on to the rim. Pump up tyre.

Points to remember

Of course there are many more jobs that you might have to tackle if you want to completely maintain your bicycle yourself, but this isn't a workshop manual, just a basic guide.

Here are some points to remember when considering how to keep your bicycle in top condition.

1 If your brakes don't engage and release easily, then the problem is almost certainly a fraying cable. Replace it.

2 Keep your brakes adjusted so that you don't have to pull a lot on the levers before they take effect.

3 If you have a leather saddle, watch for it sagging in the middle and the sides splaying out. If this happens, then tighten the leather tension by means of the nut under the nose of the saddle.

4 Attend to any problems with wheels and tyres as soon as possible. Buckled wheels should be trued, and the rim replaced if it has taken such a knock that there is a 'flat' in its surface. Check frequently that the wheels run true. You can do this by spinning the wheel and keeping your eyes on a fixed point, such as one brake block, and seeing if the rim of the wheel appears to move closer or further away from the block as it spins. Take the wheel to a repair shop if there is a problem. Bulges or warps in an outer cover of a tyre are warnings of imminent tyre-bursts, so replace the cover.

5 Check regularly the tightness of every nut and bolt.

Fault finder

Symptom	Problem	Solution
'Juddering' when front brake is applied	Badly buckled rim	Almost certain replacement of rim but cycle shop may be able to correct.
	or Loose front brake	Tighten control bolt at rear of fork crown.
	or Loose headset	Slacken locknut at top of headset, tighten top race on ball bearings with fingers, re-tighten locknut. If forks don't move smoothly round, you've overdone it, so reverse the operation slightly. If forks are tight in places, loose in others, you probably need new ball bearings or a complete new headset.
One brake block refuses to move away from the rim when the brake is released.	Brake not centred	Try slackening off centre bolt from the rear of fork crown, centre brake so that brake blocks are same distance from rim each side, then re-tighten.
	or Brake spring not equally tensioned	Put end of screwdriver across coiled (top) part of spring on the opposite side of centre bolt to the sticking brake block. Tap top of screwdriver sharply with hammer. Try again, then repeat operation until spring operates equally both sides.
Brake lever pulls right up to handlebars.	Cable too slack	If adjuster exists at brake lever or on brake stirrup, use it until enough slack is taken up. If not then slacken nut clamping cable to brake stirrup, pinch stirrups slightly together, then re-tighten cable clamp nut again. This is a trial and error operation, and fortunately most brakes now have adjusters.
Gear lever on derailleur moves without any consequent movement to front or rear machanism.	Cable too slack	Virtually as above, but few rear gears and no front gears have adjusters. So slacken off the cable clamping nut on the front changer or rear gear, whichever appropriate, pull cable tight with pliers, and re-tighten.
Rear gear moves into spokes or makes chain drop between smallest sprocket and frame. Or fails to change into top or bottom gear.	Lateral throw wrongly adjusted	The sideways movement of a rear derailleur gear (and the front changer, come to that) is controlled by two screws which, as they are loosened or tightened, allow more or less travel of the mechanism. Taken to extremes, this means tightening both screws could fix you firmly in middle gear. Look at your mechanism and you can see, as the gear moves, which screw works on the 'top' end of the range, which on the 'bottom'. Then adjust as necessary.
Chain jumps.	Is it an old chain on a new freewheel?	Replace chain.
	or Stiff link	Check each link for stiffness, then ease with chain-link extractor tool.

TOURING

One of the delights of cycling is that a bicycle not only gets you somewhere, but also allows you to enjoy yourself on the way.

Cycle touring is a fascinating way of spending leisure time, and it combines with so many other hobbies. You can be a cycle tourist, and at the same time be a photographer, fisherman, bird-watcher, geologist, what you will. Cycling along at a comfortable speed enables you to appreciate the countryside you're passing through. A cyclist makes hardly any noise, so, unlike a car, doesn't frighten away wild anim-als and birds. A cyclist is moving slowly enough to absorb the sights, sounds and smells of the country, and can stop when he or she wants – no parking problems, no fuss, no bother. And a cyclist doesn't run out of petrol either!

Gears

The section on choosing a bicycle will tell you what kind of bicycle you'll need to enjoy cycle touring – either a sports bicycle with a good saddlebag, or a machine

▷ Low gears, big mountains. Cycle touring can take you far afield; and remember – there are as many freewheels down the hills as there are climbs.

specially built for touring. Make sure that your gear range is right for the kind of country you'll be tackling, with plenty of low gears if you're going into hilly terrain. It's better to have gears that are on the low side than to be struggling along trying to push gears that are far too high. With a chainwheel of between 46 and 52 teeth you'll need a largest rear sprocket of 28 teeth, for example, if you want to tackle really tough climbs. In normal countryside, providing you're not heavily loaded, you can get by with a 22 or 24. It's a simple matter for your cycle dealer to change a freewheel sprocket or even the whole freewheel if necessary.

Clothes

What about clothing? Obviously you'll dress for the temperature, but remember that when you're riding along, the breeze has a cooling effect, and even in comparatively warm weather you might be glad of a windproof jacket over the top of your shirt, tee shirt or sweater. But try not to use a nylon windproof; because they make you sweat a lot, quite unnecessarily.

On a hot day there's nothing nicer than freewheeling down a hill, cooled by the breeze in your hair; but it's a good idea always to remember your suntan lotion, and wear a teeshirt and even a cotton cap. On the open road you are very exposed to the sun beating down, and if you're concentrating on pedalling you may not notice how hot it's getting. At the end of the day you may discover your back burning and you've got a headache from the sun. It might be a good way of getting a tan, but you can spoil a

◁ Dressed for spring or autumn touring. Note the long socks, the 'plus two' trousers, the light cycle shoes.

△ The annual
London–Brighton
ride is a great day out
for racers, potterers and
families alike.

▷ Shorts and a
jersey are ideal
wear for touring in
summer – the jersey
can always be taken off
if you get too hot.

whole holiday with a single day's riding without protection. Even sunburnt knees or elbows can be extremely uncomfortable when you get back on the bike next day.

You can wear shorts if it's warm, but they should be of a good material with 'body', such as cord, twill or worsted. No football shorts please – they're too flimsy, and can bunch up between your legs and make you sore. The same goes for under-wear; it should be a close fit, and not gather where you sit on the saddle.

You can wear any kind of trousers for cycling, of course, providing you keep them out of the way of the chain, but there are special trousers made for cycling, which have a double seat, to guard against the saddle wearing through the material.

The cut allows you to pedal easily without any tightness over

△ Modern panniers and bags are neat and capacious; if you pack them properly you won't affect the bike's handling.

version of grandfather's golfing trousers (the 'plus fours' of years ago); or a more normal trouser which is tapered from the knee, rather like a tracksuit, and has zips at the ankles. The close fit over the lower leg means you don't need to worry about trouser clips.

With the 'plus twos' you would wear knee-length socks, while any ankle sock can be worn with tapered cycling trousers.

Again, you can wear normal town shoes for cycling, and they are better, because of their stiffer sole, than gym shoes, or the 'training' shoes you can buy, which have thick rubber soles. But if you want to feel properly kitted out for touring, then you can buy quite inexpensive cycling shoes, which are a close fit, will have a lightweight heel (so you can walk in them if necessary), and fit nicely into toe-clips and straps, which you will probably have fitted if you're serious about cycling.

There are even special 'shoe-plates' which make pedalling even easier. Made of metal or strong plastics, they are nailed or screwed to the sole, and have a slot into which the rear plate of a metal pedal fits, giving a more positive pedalling action. The only drawback is that walking on shoe-plates isn't very comfortable.

'Track mitts' – fingerless gloves, usually with a leather palm and a string or crocheted back – are another worthwhile item of cycling clothing. They guard against sore hands when you're riding long distances, and offer protection if you're unlucky enough to take a tumble, when you invariably stretch out your hands to break your fall.

the knees, and gives you plenty of coverage for the lower back, where it's all too easy for a gap to appear when a normal sweater and trousers are worn. That strip of bare flesh is a target for cold air, and you can catch a chill as a result.

There are two styles of cycling trousers, either 'plus twos', which finish just below the knee with a piece of ribbed elastic or woolly fabric, rather like a modern

Maps

You've got your bicycle ready, you're kitted out for the job – where are you going? Answering this question, planning where to go, how to get there, where to stop along the way, can be almost as much fun as carrying out your plans.

Whether you're going away for a long day's ride or a three-week tour, you need to plan carefully.

The first essential is maps. You can plan roughly where you're going on a large-scale map, such as the route-planning maps used by motorists. But for detailed planning, and to take with you, it's best to use smaller scale maps, such as one or two centimetres to the kilometre, or half or one inch to the mile.

Maps tell you much more than the right roads to take. They give information on the size of towns and villages, the locations of youth hostels, inns, post offices and places of historic interest. They can help you work out whether the cycling is likely to be easy or hard, through either colour contours (changing from the dark green of low-lying land through to the brown of hills and the grey of mountains), or contour lines, which link places of equal height.

If contour lines are far apart, then the countryside is flat. If they're close together, then prepare for steep gradients.

Even the roads themselves are described on maps, allowing you to choose routes on secondary roads likely to be free of heavy traffic.

The first step in route planning is to decide on the area of your ride or tour. If it's a day run, then you'll know roughly how far you can venture before you turn back, but perhaps you've not considered the idea of taking the train for some distance, and starting your ride on new roads quite a distance away from home.

◁ A useful accessory is a handlebar bag with a transparent map pocket, which makes finding your way a simpler process.

It's fun to use maps to discover where you are – and where you should go next.

Taking your bicycle on the train is usually free in Britain (except for a few intercity services). Normally cycles are accepted on local trains, but not always on mainline routes; if you have any doubts about this, check with British Rail when you are planning your tour.

You do not need a special ticket to take a bicycle on a train in Britain. Write out a luggage label, with your name and address, and the stations you are travelling to and from, then take the bike to the guard. He or she will put it in the guard's van (or let you do it yourself, which is better since you can check that it's safe and won't fall over). Remind the guard of your destination; then, when you get there, ask him to get it out for you.

In trains without a guard's van, you have to keep the bike in the passenger compartment with you. In this case remember to keep it out of the way of other passengers as much as you can.

On the Continent it's a bit more complicated. Bicycles travel as parcels, which means that you have to hand them in to the parcels office at the station of departure, and pay for them. Usually the office can't guarantee which train the bike will be put on; only that it will arrive as soon as possible. For some reason they always seem to need several hours notice to put any bike on any train. So you have to travel separated from your bike and probably wait for it for hours at the other end.

If your journey involves any complicated changes of train this can prove nerve-racking. Suppose you want to go to central or southern France. You can take your bike on the ferry across the Channel all right, riding it on and off the boat (usually overtaking long queues of fuming motorists in the process). Then you might have to take a train to one terminus in Paris, cross the city and pick up your connection at another. It's not the easiest procedure even for a passenger to follow; but it's a lot worse for your bike without you to point it in the right direction! If you are thinking of a tour that might involve this sort of complicated change, be sure to check up with the national rail network before you leave home.

Once you've decided on the area, then go to a library or bookshop and find guidebooks to give you more information about where you're going – you might find it worthwhile making a detour to visit the birthplace or former house of a famous personality, or the site of an old battle you've read about. There could be stately homes worth visiting, wild-life parks, museums, places of outstanding natural beauty such as caves or waterfalls. A good guidebook will give you ideas galore.

So pick the places you definitely want to see, within the rough touring area you've selected, and start to work out your route between them.

Mileage

Be sensible about mileage. If you're an inexperienced cyclist, a day's ride of 50 to 65 kilometres (30 to 40 miles) can be quite enough, allowing for meal stops and time to play the sightseer. Hard riding tourists might do 130 to 160 kilometres (80 to 100 miles) in a day, but the average tends to be around 100 kilometres (60 miles).

Bear in mind the terrain too. On one of my first tours away from home I went to Devon and Cornwall, and found myself walking up so many steep hills that 65 kilometres (40 miles) a day was plenty, thank you! So underestimate the mileage you can cover; if you get to your destination earlier than expected, you can always go for a little loop around the area to add to your mileage.

And talking about loops, if you're going for a round trip from home or a touring base, then take the wind direction into account, and hope it doesn't change. Better to ride into the wind in the morning when you're fresh, and let it blow you home later, when you're tired. There's nothing worse than struggling into a headwind in the gathering gloom.

Places to stay

You'll need to work out where you are going to stay if you're away from home overnight or longer.

The first choice for the young cyclist is probably youth hostels. Controlled in England and Wales by the Youth Hostels Association (YHA), with similar bodies in Scotland, Northern Ireland and Eire, the youth hostel movement was formed with the idea of helping youngsters travelling and enjoying the countryside under their own steam: cycling, walking, canoeing, pony-trekking for instance. Nowadays school parties often use hostels, and motorists are allowed to use them too. But the traditions of hostelling remain the same, young people meeting in simple surroundings, eating and sleeping at low cost.

You should be a member of the YHA or the national youth hostelling body in your country. Membership also allows you to go to youth hostels abroad.

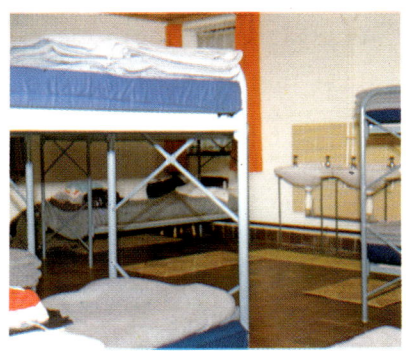

▷ A typical hostel dormitory.

◁ The outside appearances of hostels vary, from purpose-built affairs to old manor houses. This one is in France.

The type of accommodation offered by hostels varies immensely, from the large, heavily-used hostels in city centres to small, simple hostels, perhaps housing only a dozen 'bednighters', up in the mountains or on a bleak moor. The majority of hostels offer a choice of either eating hostel meals or cooking your own in the 'members' kitchen' where basic utensils are provided. In smaller hostels it's sometimes 'self-cookers only', and the warden will usually have a small stock of food for sale. You can find out exactly what facilities the hostel has by looking in the YHA handbook or its equivalent.

Sleeping accommodation is basic, on bunks in dormitories. You take or hire a sheet sleeping-bag, and make up your own bed with blankets and pillows provided. And as part of your contribution to the upkeep of the hostel, you'll probably be given a 'chore' by the warden before you leave.

There are many youth hostels in Britain and abroad, but some are very popular, so book beforehand if you can.

Maybe you prefer something a little more comfortable than youth hostels. If so, then membership of the Cyclists' Touring Club (CTC) will provide you with a handbook of 'approved' accommodation all over Britain, again at inexpensive prices, and often in small boarding houses or private homes. Anyone contemplating serious touring ought to think about joining the CTC anyway. They have local groups who organize tours and have other social activities. Head office operates a route-planning and information service for members, and other benefits include free third-party insurance and legal aid, plus an advantageous cycle insurance scheme. There are similar bodies in many other countries.

Incidentally the British Cycling Federation (BCF), the governing body of racing in England and Wales, also operates a touring service.

That gives the alternative of hostels or cheap, recommended accommodation. What's left is a choice between two extremes – hotels, which naturally present a price problem, or camping, which for many tourists has brought added enjoyment and a closer contact with the 'great outdoors'.

Camping

Nowadays, with lightweight materials, you can go cycle-camping without carrying too much luggage, and if there are two or more of you sharing the load, then life is even simpler.

A modern lightweight tent (get one with a sewn-in groundsheet and a flysheet) plus its telescopic poles and tent pegs, will fit easily into a large saddlebag, leaving plenty of room for a compact down or Terylene filled sleeping-bag, clothes, eating and cooking utensils in rear panniers.

A trip round a camping shop will introduce you to the modern aids to lightweight camping, such as nests of cooking pans, dehydrated and concentrated foods, lightweight and portable gas stoves or solid-fuel burners. The better you're equipped, the more you'll enjoy yourself.

Try to cut down as much as possible on luggage. Use several layers of thin clothes rather than one bulky one. They will be warmer and will take less room in the saddlebag. If you're taking provisions, use containers big enough only for what you need – a small screw-top plastic or metal sugar-tin, never a whole packet, for instance. Take clothing in drip-dry materials and wash them, rather than taking enough changes to last you through a tour.

Riding with friends

It may be that you're a loner, someone who likes cycling on their own; but it's most likely that some time during your cycling career you'll be riding with other people.

Having someone riding along-side you is a pleasurable experience. You've got company, conversation, often a cheering word to make the difference when you're feeling tired. If you

Touring Checklist

If you are thinking of going on a camping holiday by bicycle this list will give you some idea of what equipment you will need to buy or borrow, and it will provide a final checklist so you can make sure you haven't forgotten any essentials!

pannier bags
handlebar bag
lightweight tent
groundsheet
sleeping bag
cotton sheet lining for sleeping bag
cooking stove

fuel for stove
simple cooking canteen or nest of pans
mug and deep plate
knife, fork and spoon
can opener
matches in waterproof container
water carrier (collapsible ones are available)
small tins of salt, sugar, tea, coffee and dried milk

suitable clothes (see text) including one complete change of clothing
track mitts
towel
toilet bag including soap etc.
swimming gear

◁ If you want to have an enjoyable and successful cycle camping holiday, choose your tent and cooking equipment carefully.

washing powder
waterproof cape or waterproof
    jacket and trousers

maps and compass
YHA membership card
wallet
notebook and pencil
camera
first aid kit
glucose tablets/chocolate
pocket knife
torch
tool kit
puncture repair kit
spare inner tube
lamps – front and rear and spare
    batteries
pump
cycle lock
length of nylon cord and pegs for
    guying bicycle upright

If this equipment sounds rather difficult to pack on a bicycle remember that if two or more of you travel together you can share the weight of the tent and cooking equipment, and today's lightweight equipment means that weight should not be a problem.

Remember to pack so that things you may need quickly – like your wallet, the first aid kit, waterproofs, maps, etc. – are easily reached.

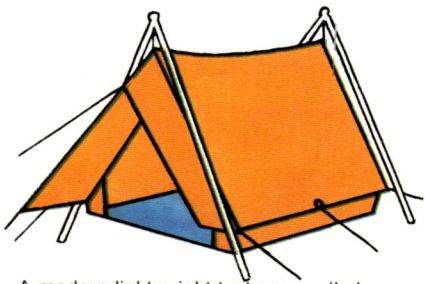

A modern lightweight tent can easily be carried on a bicycle.

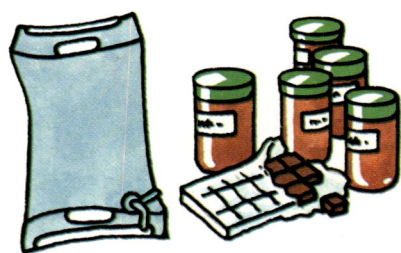

A plastic water carrier is a great help, and a selection of foodstuffs is useful in case you camp away from shops.

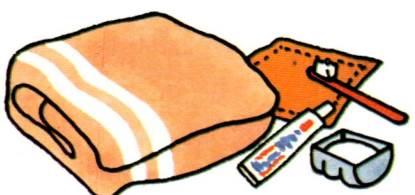

Don't forget towel and washing gear.

Check that the sleeping bag and stove you choose weigh as little as possible.

Maps, a compass and a penknife with gadgets are useful aids which you should keep within easy reach.

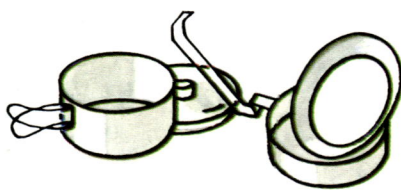

Look for stacking pans with removable handles to save space.

Take only the basic, essential crockery and cutlery.

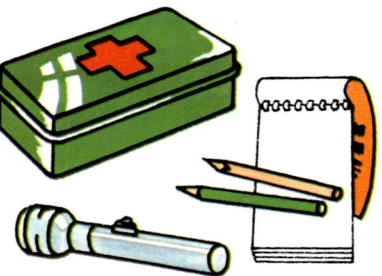

A first aid kit, a torch and a notebook and pencil should also be packed at the top of your panniers.

You don't always follow tarmac roads on club runs. Good tracks can fill the bill.

Even streamlining can be a help sometimes!

join a cycling club then you'll be going on 'club runs', and you'll find that, riding in pairs and each pair taking a turn at the front of the double file, the miles roll under your wheels faster than they would do if you rode alone. Riding behind someone else means that you are being sheltered from the wind, which means you use less energy to go at a given speed.

But riding in company means a responsibility to your companions. Changes of direction should be signalled to the riders behind you, just as you'll get them from the riders in front: 'Going left!' the front man might shout, and the cry is taken up down the column.

Similarly, road hazards like parked cars, glass on the road or potholes in it should be the subject of warnings. 'Easy!' goes the shout, and that means someone up front is slowing down, either to stop eventually, or to negotiate some hazard.

In well-organized group rides the double column of riders seems like a serpent, snaking its way along, instead of a number of individuals riding together. There should be no sudden manoeuvres such as sharp braking or sudden changes in direction, and every consideration should be given to other road users, such as overtaking cars, and especially horses and their riders. Cyclists have their right to a place on the road, but it is bad manners and often unsafe not to ride in single file on narrow or winding roads.

Cycling in a group can be great

Pleasure riding enthusiasts in the USA adopt their own styles of dress and equipment.

fun, with the occasional 'dig' on a hill to see who the strongest might be, adding a dash of the competitive. Stopping for 'elevenses' lunch or tea is a chance for yarn-swapping. You often learn more about cycling over a meal-table with experienced cyclists than you do in years riding on your own.

Guidelines for the tourist

Always dress well: wear just enough clothes to feel warm, but not so many that you start to sweat profusely just riding normally. If you're perspiring because of climbing a steep hill, don't take off any clothes at the top to cool down; the descent will see to that, and it might even be worth donning an extra sweater if the descent is a long one. Don't let sweat cool on you if you can help it. It's no hardship to carry a small towel and dry off – especially the small of your back – when you stop. In cold weather, look after your extremities: hands in gloves with wrists

covered, feet in thicker socks, head covered with a cap or woolly hat.

Don't carry anything on yourself if you can carry it on the bicycle. If you aren't riding with a saddlebag, resist the temptation to fill a musette with tools, spare and cape, and sling the bag on your back. Better to strap them all under the saddle.

Always carry food and drink if you're out for more than about 90 minutes. A muesli bar, orange or glucose tablets can work wonders if you're tired, and fruit juice, glucose drinks – even cold tea (without milk) can also be wonderfully refreshing.

Sometime in your cycling life you'll experience the feeling that cyclists variously call the 'bonk', 'knock', or 'a packet'. In simple terms, your body has run out of energy, and suddenly your legs feel weak, your head light, and you find that even pedalling slowly is an immense effort. The remedy is to eat something sweet as quickly as possible. It's amazing how quickly you recover – and it's a good, if drastic way, to learn why you should carry food

You should do some training before you set off on a long tour heavily laden.

with you on anything but a very short ride.

Carry enough tools to solve any minor repair problems. A box or adjustable spanner, screwdriver, puncture outfit (and spare tube if on a long ride) take up little room, and you may have cause to bless them. If you are caught out, then try a garage for help. Always carry a small first aid kit for cuts, bruises and stings.

◁ Beware: camels crossing! North African touring has extra problems for the intrepid cyclist.

Pedal briskly, using the gear which allows you to turn it at between 80 and 100 revs per minute. Using big gears and turning them slowly is less economical, in energy terms, than turning a small gear much faster. Change down for hills and try to pedal up them without leaving the saddle if you can. Standing up on the pedals (known as 'honking', for some reason) is a strong man's way of climbing hills which uses up a lot of energy.

When you brake, do it gradually and smoothly, preferably using both brakes. On bends, especially downhill, do your braking before you change direction, so you are in more control when you actually negotiate the bend itself.

Don't be stupid about lights. If there's even a faint chance of being on the road after the daylight starts to fade, then take lights with you, and make sure they work well.

CYCLING AS A SPORT

Cycle racing, like athletics, has different events for different talents. Some suit the rider who has a blistering but short-lived burst of speed, others the one who can ride steadily for hours on end; still others the cunning or agile rider whose tactical knowledge

▷ Racing is usually done in teams, with members helping each other to find top speed.

A tough European classic race, involving some of the world's best riders over a gruelling course.

and skill enables him to preserve his energies while others are expending theirs.

Some events are on tracks specially built for cycle racing, others on public roads, still others use fields and paths.

The main divisions of cycling racing are road racing, time trialling, track racing and cyclocross. Cyclo-cross takes place in winter, in Britain from the end of September to mid-February, while the road and time trial season extends from February to November, with outdoor track racing from Easter until September.

Let's look at road racing first, because this is the kind of competition which draws the crowds and has an enormous following throughout the world and especially in Europe.

Road racing

Generally road racing is a very simple type of event, with all the competitors starting together, racing a given course, with the first one over the finishing line winning.

Most road races are just like this, taking place either on a largish circuit of 16 kilometres

Road racing is not just for boys and men – there are races for girls and women at all levels. And there are many keen female competitors.

(ten miles) or so, or on a route from place to place.

Races from town to town can vary in distance from about 50 kilometres (30 miles), to more than 160 kilometres (100 miles) for the best amateurs and 240 kilometres (150 miles) and more for professionals. Average speeds are around 40 kph (25 mph).

During a road race there might be several intermediate prizes, called *primes* (pronounced 'pre-ems'). Prime is the French word for bonus, and this is what it is, a bonus to the finishing prize list, perhaps for a sprint at a given point or points during the race, or for the first man over a difficult hill climb. Some events have a 'King of the Mountains' prize for the best hill-climber, awarded no matter what his finishing position might be.

Road races are controlled by a commissaire – a judge who travels in a car with the race, and watches for rule infringements. Most road races, and all the big ones, are followed by service cars, which carry spare bicycles and wheels to help out riders in trouble. In professional or amateur international events there is usually a service car for every team.

Although road races are essentially individual events, team racing does play a part. If a rider punctures, his team-mates will often drop back from the main field to pace him back to the leaders after the service car has done its work. If one team member is a strong sprinter, his team-mates will 'nurse' him to the finish, keeping him sheltered from the wind until the finishing sprint.

Similarly, if a team's best rider has broken away alone or in a small group, his team-mates will

△ The start of a road race involves a lot of jockeying for position.

go to the front of the main field (the 'bunch') and try to slow down any chase which might start, so that their leader can increase his advantage. In contrast, if a rival team has a man away in the leading group, they will take turns at the front of the field whipping up the chase, until the breakaway has been recaptured.

So you can see that road racing is not just a mad 'blind' from the dropping of the flag to the finish line, but often a highly tactical affair. One great French road racing expert used to say that a real champion needed *la tête et les jambes* – the head and the legs – because pedalling was only part of being a good roadman.

Stage races

Apart from simple one-day road races, there are stage races, which extend from two days, to, in the case of the Tour de France, more than three weeks. Each day there is a race with a winner, but riders' times on each daily 'stage' are also totalled to produce an overall leader at any stage, and a winner at the end.

Stage races are not just a succession of daily road races; they include individual time trials and team time trials as well.

In stage races a rider must finish a certain stage of the race each day to be allowed to start the next.

The race leader on any particular stage is distinguished by wearing a special jersey. Most famous of these is the yellow jersey worn by the leader in the Tour de France. Britain's Milk Race is one of many other events whose race leader is also in yellow.

Stage races can be either from town to town to town (in which

▷ Race leader in the Tour de France wearing the famous yellow jersey.

The Tour de France
passes through .

Sprinting for the finishing line.

case they might be given the misleading name of 'tours') or all the stages can start and finish from the same place.

The handicap

Another variation of a road race is called a handicap, and this is designed to give a winning chance to everybody. The winner is still the first one across the finishing line, but the start is 'staggered'. The slowest riders are started first, the fastest last, and theoretically, if the handicap has been fair, everyone should finish together. The judges are usually thankful that it doesn't happen that way!

Small circuit events

Some road events are specially designed for the spectator, because they use small circuits, sometimes as short as 550 metres (600 yards) but usually around 1·6 kilometres (a mile). This means the race is in view every minute or two, bringing the action to the public. There are two types of small circuit event, the *criterium*, which takes place entirely on a small circuit, and a *kermesse* (the French word for a market) which is usually held at the time of a local market or fair and starts and finishes on a small spectator-jammed circuit, taking in a bigger circuit in between.

Small circuit events demand agility and daring. There are bends and sharp corners to be negotiated every few seconds, and a rider who can take a corner 'at its limit', leaning his bicycle over until his pedals are almost scraping the road surface, can gain steadily on another, less adventurous rider, who might be faster on a straight-out test of speed and stamina.

Naturally these events are

Small circuit racing involves good cornering. Note how all these youngsters corner with their inside knee raised.

favourites with the crowds. The corners add a touch of danger, and there are sometimes crashes when someone takes too much of a chance – with normally no more serious result than a few bruises.

A European kermesse is a great experience for a spectator, with an almost unbroken stream of action on the circuit, and an enthusiastic commentator not only sorting out where and who the leaders are, but also persuading the spectators to put up money – *primes* – to spur on the riders to even greater efforts. The prime money doesn't always go to the leaders; sometimes it is used to give a chasing group something extra to ride for, so there is always something interesting to watch.

The criterium is a regular feature of cycling life in France, Belgium and Italy, the world's three major cycle racing nations.

It is also becoming more common in Britain, thanks, largely, to the series of 'city-centre cycling' races sponsored by Kellogg's and Channel 4 television. For the past few years, six of these races have been held in big cities around Britain and leading professional British, Australian and continental riders have competed.

Usually the race is for an hour, with several primes or sprint laps interspersed throughout it. Points are awarded for a win or for placings, and the overall winner is the rider with the most points over the series of six races. These races have attracted larger and larger crowds each year, and have really helped to bring cycle racing to the forefront of public attention. After the race you may get a chance to mingle with the riders, look over their bicycles and get a taste of what professional cycling is all about.

△ The Kellogg's/
Channel 4 City
Centre races have put
cycle racing on the map
in Britain.

◁ Start of a Bath to
London cycle race,
at the end of the last
century.

Time trialling

On the last day of May 1868, the first recorded cycle race took place, at St Cloud in France, and was won by James Moore from Britain.

From that time onwards, racing of all kinds took a quick hold on the imagination of fans in Britain, France, and the USA. Many cycle tracks were built, and racing on public roads became widespread. But whereas in Europe the sport became more and more popular, it had a setback in Britain when, during the last years of the 19th century, police objections to racing on the open road grew steadily until cycle racing on roads was finally banned.

The competitive urge is not so easily blunted however. Racing enthusiasts reasoned that a British citizen had the right to ride on British roads. As long as he was alone, and not battling elbow-to-elbow with another rider, why should he not ride over a given couse, as fast as he could? And if a lot of cyclists felt they wanted to ride over the same course at about the same time, what could possibly be wrong with that?

In this way time trialling was born, a way of racing on the

◁ Training for the big race involves many hours of hard work for months.

roads without causing problems for other road users.

In the beginning, the time triallists were very careful not to draw attention to themselves and their activities. The details of the events were kept 'private and confidential'; riders had to wear inconspicuous clothing which amounted to black tights and a black jacket, a far cry from the shorts and multi-coloured jerseys of today. Events were held early in the morning, almost always on Sundays, with no great spectacle, just a number of individual riders pedalling along the road, having been started at a time interval, usually of one minute.

Although riders now ride in much more eye-catching clothes, and although there are races in the evenings, Saturday afternoons and Sundays and it's easy to discover where and when events take place nowadays, the principle of time trialling hasn't changed.

Restrictions on bunched racing on British roads disappeared

SOME CYCLING RECORDS

WORLD RECORDS
Unpaced standing start
Men

1,000m	1 min 02.9 sec	L. Thoms	1980
5,000m	5 min 45.6 sec	H. H. Oersted	1985
10,000m	11 min 39.7 sec	F. Moser	1984
100km	2 hr 14 min 02 sec	O. Ritter	1971
1 hour	51.15km	F. Moser	1984
24 hour (track)	830km	M. Secrest	1985
1,000 miles	51 hr 12 min 32 sec	H. de Munck	1983

Motor-paced

100km	1 hr 12 min 04 sec	M. Hurzeler	1984
1 hour	90.48km	A. Romanov	1985

Women

1,000m	1 min 13.4 sec	E. Salumyae	1983
5,000m	6 min 41.7 sec	A. Jones	1982
10,000m	13 min 34.4 sec	K. Van Oostenhage	1978
100km	2 hr 31 min 28 sec	F. Galli	1985
1 hour	43.08km`	K. Van Oostenhage	1978

BRITISH RECORDS
Road cycling
Men

10 miles	19 min 11 sec	D. Lloyd	1981
25 miles	49 min 24 sec	A. Engers	1978
50 miles	1 hr 39 min 51 sec	I. Cammish	1983
12 hours	287.3 miles	G. Longland	1983
24 hours	507 miles	R. Cromack	1969
London to Edinburgh (380 miles)	18 hr 49 min 42 sec	C. Smith	1965
London to Brighton and back (107 miles)	4 hr 15 min 08 sec	P. Griffiths	1977
Land's End to London (287 miles)	12 hr 34 min	R. Maitland	1954
Land's End to John o' Groats (847 miles)	45 hr 3 min 16 sec	J. Woodburn	1982

Women

10 miles	21 min 25 sec	B. Burton	1973
25 miles	53 min 21 sec	B. Burton	1976
50 miles	1 hr 51 min 30 sec	B. Burton	1976
12 hours	277.25 miles	B. Burton	1967
24 hours	438 miles	A. Mann	1983
Land's End to John o' Groats (847 miles)	59 hr 11 min 7 sec	E. Sheridan	1954

soon after the Second World War, but time trialling continued to flourish even though the reason for its creation no longer applied.

Although time trialling doesn't provide man-to-man competition, it offers something which road racing never can. Because most events are over standard distances, and courses are normally 'out and home',

The shortest type of time trial, a hill climb. This rider favours a fixed wheel.

thus cancelling out any wind advantage, one rider in, say, Cornwall, can effectively compare his times with someone in Newcastle.

Similarly, a rider without a hope of winning an event can still derive pleasure from attempting to beat his own 'personal bests'.

Time trialling in Britain today is under the control of the Road Time Trials Council in England and Wales, and the Scottish Cyclists' Union in Scotland. There are time trials in virtually every cycle racing country, but nowhere are they as popular as in Britain.

Although some time trials are over hilly, twisted courses, aimed at testing bike-handling ability as well as speed, the majority are over standard distances: 10, 25, 50 and 100 miles (16, 40, 80 and 160 kilometres). Courses are usually on flat roads, with the start and finish near one another, to minimize the effect of the wind.

Events are cheap to enter, and as long as a rider is a member of a club affiliated to the governing body, then he needs no licence. Start sheets list entered riders who start at their appointed time and ride the appointed course. Riders start at minute intervals, and in this way overtaking is kept to a minimum. If one rider does catch another up, then the code of conduct is that neither rider should take pace from the other.

Younger riders aren't encouraged to tackle the longer distances, and most wait until they turn senior (18 years old) before tackling anything longer than 25 miles (40 kilometres).

The problem with time trialling is to pace yourself so that by the finish your energy is just about used up – not to take things too easily nor to start so fast that you run out of legs before you get back to the timekeeper.

Most time trials are individual, but some, especially early in the season, are for teams. Team time trials can be for two, three, four or even more riders in every team. The aim is to get enough of the team (two or three if three or four start) to the finish as quickly as possible, and this is achieved by each rider taking a short turn in the lead, sheltering the others from the wind, and then dropping to the back.

The shortest time trials are hill climbs, which can last even less than a minute, but which, for the enthusiastic participants, can be just as exhausting as a much longer race.

Road record-breaking

There is one other form of riding 'alone and unpaced' which is again peculiarly British. This is road record-breaking, governed in England by the Road Records Association, and with other bodies governing Welsh, Scottish and regional records.

These bodies set out to organize and verify the fastest rides over given distances, or from one nominated place to another. These rides are not to be done in time trials, but when the would-be record-breaker is alone on his chosen road.

Existing records range from 25 miles (40 kilometres) to 1,000 miles (1,600 kilometres), and place-to-place records include London to Brighton and back, and the 'End to End', from one end of Britain to the other – Land's End to John O'Groats – for which the record was brought inside two days in 1965.

Anyone can attack a road record, but they have first to notify the governing body, which sends out observers to check that the rules are adhered to.

Track racing

Another major division of cycle racing is the track. There are many kinds of cycle track in the world, from the 150 metre tightly-banked wooden, 'wall of death' indoor track to some tracks which are almost flat and measure about 550 metres (600 yards). The only essentials for a

The steeply-banked indoor wooden track used for the London six-day race.

The start of a grass-track event.

cycle racing track are a hard surface, be it wood, asphalt or concrete, and enough banking to help the riders to round the bends without losing speed.

In practice, indoor tracks are between 150 and 250 metres (164 and 273 yards), with most good outdoor tracks between 250 and 400 metres (273 and 437 yards). The Munich and Montreal Olympic tracks both measure 285 metres (312 yards), and the track at Leicester, on which Britain organized the 1970 world championships measures 333 metres (364 yards).

Let's take a look at the various events you might see at a track meeting, where the events can be as varied as those at an atheltics meet.

The sprint

Most straightforward of all is the sprint event, for between two and six riders normally, depending on the width of the track.

The first man over the finish line wins, but this doesn't mean that everyone goes flat out from the starting gun. Instead, there is often a lot of tactical riding. At high speed, a rider following

A flattish outdoor hard track, featuring a bunched race.

▷ Tactics in a sprint race. Both riders are moving slowly, the leader keeping an eye out for a surprise move by the second rider.

immediately behind another is sheltered from the wind, and can conserve his strength.

So in sprint events most riders try to get the back position, tucked neatly in their opponent's slipstream until a late stage, when they try to overtake and win, using the energy they've saved by better positioning.

This is why, quite often, you get riders on a 'go slow', each one trying to force the other to take the lead. Sometimes experienced riders can make their bicycles stand still for many minutes until they gain the position they want. One tactic to combat a standstill is not only to take the lead, but to make a surprise effort, gaining so much ground before the other rider reacts that he cannot possibly catch up.

The sprint is the fastest un-paced cycling event, with speeds of up to 72 kph (45 mph) sometimes recorded over the last 200 metres (218 yards), which is

▷ Team pursuiting – the front rider takes his turn, then moves to the back to rest.

the normal timed portion.

There are also tandem sprint events, which are similar, except for higher speeds and a smaller number of standstills, which are far more difficult on a 'twicer'.

The track handicap

Another fast event is the handicap, where slower riders are given a start on the faster ones. Handicaps can be very short, perhaps 500 metres (547 yards), or over three kilometres (two miles).

The scratch and the points race

There are two kinds of race where a big field starts together, the scratch race and the points race. In a scratch race the first man across the line wins; in a

points race there are points awarded for sprints at various times during the race, usually every lap on an outdoor track. The rider amassing the biggest points total wins.

The 'Devil'

Not necessarily a fast race, but definitely fun for the spectators, is the 'Devil', short for 'Devil take the Hindmost'. Also called a 'Miss 'n Out' in the USA, this event starts with a bunch of riders, and the last rider (or sometimes two riders) over the line at designated times, usually every lap, is eliminated. This goes on until there are perhaps two to four riders left on the track, and they decide the final placings in a sprint. The knack is not so much in going fast, but in keeping out of danger for the opening laps, saving your speed for later.

The kilometre time trial

One classic test of speed and an Olympic event, is the kilometre time trial. Competitors ride a kilometre from a standing start, alone, and in turn. The fastest time wins, and this is usually just over a minute.

The pursuit race

Another favourite with the crowd, especially if the riders are well matched, is the pursuit race. Normally two riders start on opposite sides of the track and 'pursue' one another for the distance of the race, usually 4,000 or 5,000 metres (4,374 or 5,468 yards). If one rider catches the other within the distance, then he wins automatically. Otherwise, the fastest time wins. Sometimes a rider with a fast start but no staying-power will try to catch his opponent in the early laps, before his strength runs out. Because the pursuit needs to be so finely judged – a 4,000 metre race only lasts about five minutes – there can be surprising changes in the closing laps, so a rider who is apparently a long way behind at the halfway stage is not necessarily a loser.

One variety of this event is the station pursuit (called by some the Australian pursuit). In this event there are more than two riders (sometimes as many as eight), spaced equally round the track. The principle is the same, but there is even more excitement as the slow starters try to stay clear of the fast starters not so far behind them!

The other pursuit event is the team pursuit, where two teams of four battle it out, with – just like a team time trial – each rider taking a short turn on the front, then dropping to the back of the quartet to recuperate. In a four man team pursuit, the time is taken when the third man crosses the finishing line.

Motor-paced racing

You already know about slip-streaming, which is used in road racing and in track racing when one rider wants to take advantage of another as a wind-break. In motor-paced racing this effect is even more important.

Each rider is paced by a motorcycle, sometimes just a specialized moped called a Derny but more usually (and in world championships) by a big motor-bike, with a frame extending backwards on which a roller is mounted. The cyclist will ride as close behind the pacing motor as he can, but he is limited by the position of the roller – and this is

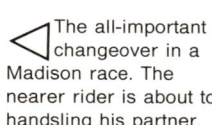

The all-important changeover in a Madison race. The nearer rider is about to handsling his partner.

△ High-speed effort
in a motor-paced
track race.

a safety factor too, because if the front tyre catches it, it simply revolves harmlessly. Pace-following riders, often called 'stayers', ride machines with small front wheels and reversed forks, to allow them to make most use of their pacemakers' shelter.

The actual racing itself is simple, the first man across the line winning. But tactics can play a big part, and the 'airwaves' set up by the riders and their pacers, moving at 80 kph (50 mph) and more, can be used to upset a rider who tries to overtake.

The Madison

One of the most spectacular – yet often confusing – events is known as the Madison, so called because it gained great popularity in New York's Madison Square Garden Stadium.

It is a kind of continuous two-man relay, most at home on a small track. One man will race, his team-mate resting by riding slowly around the upper part of the track. When the racing man wants to take a breather, he grabs his partner by the hand or the seat of his shorts and slings him into action, imparting his own momentum, and slowing down himself at the same time.

The big aim in a Madison event is to gain a full lap's lead on the other teams. If one team has a lap advantage on the rest at the end of the race, then they automatically win. If teams are equal on laps covered, then their positions are usually decided on points given for intermediate sprints.

The Madison is the basis of six-day races, normally professional events which take place during the winter season (September-February) on indoor tracks in many European cities and in Canada and Australia.

The 'Six'
A 'Six' is no longer what it used to be, literally an endurance track

race which lasted six days and nights. Nowadays most Sixes involve only six evenings or afternoons and evenings, with a racing programme designed to please the public, and often additional entertainment such as music, dancers, singers (plus good food and drink) to keep the spectators happy.

Sixes are contested by teams of

▷ A changeover in the Madison – the push method.

two or occasionally three riders, who ride Madisons, spirits, Devils, points races and time trials during the event. Like a Madison, the victory goes to any team leading by a lap or more at the end, but equal positions on laps are separated by points scores from the 'supporting events'.

Naturally riding so many different kinds of events over six days calls for riders of great all-round ability. And each team has its back-up helpers: a mechanic, a runner to bring food, see to laundry, take away rubbish, and a 'soigneur' who massages tired legs, deals with any minor ailments, and advises on tactics.

Cyclo-cross

The smooth, glittering scene of six-day racing has its exact opposite in cyclo-cross, a type of racing which calls for speed, stamina and daring – not to mention a strong bicycle!

As its name suggests, cyclo-cross is cross-country cycling – except that on some courses you just can't cycle all the time – you

◁ Gruelling winter racing. Top cyclo-cross riders during a world championship choose to carry their bicycles up this incline.

BMX races are as
fiercely competed as
anything on larger
wheels.

have to pick up your bicycle and run with it.

A typical course will include grassland, slippery paths, perhaps a stream crossing, steep run-ups and near-vertical descents. A good cyclo-cross rider will be a strong runner and a good bike-handler. He will have a good eye for the course, knowing when it's faster to ride and when running would be quicker and easier.

Cyclo-cross races are like road races, in that the field starts together and the winner is the rider first over the line at the end.

Cyclo-cross racing was done for years before anyone thought of BMX and mountain bikes. But the arrival of these specialized machines has dramatically increased the popularity of off-road racing.

BMX racing

BMX racing is mainly for kids, though it's true that there are professionals in their 20s and 30s making a good living at the sport. But saying it is for kids doesn't mean that it isn't real cycle racing, or real competition. The track, which just has a dirt surface, is usually about 300 metres (330 yards) long, incorporating a ramp at the start, banked bends, several speed bumps, flat, raised 'table-tops' and a sudden descent before the finish. Eight riders race at a time, normally graded by age, and competitors need all their skill at handling their machines, cornering, skidding, jumping and hopping, as well as sheer speed and courage to come out on top. Protective gear, including helmet with mouthpiece, gloves, knee-

and elbow-pads, are essential.

In 1986 the BMX world championships were held in Slough, Buckinghamshire. Almost 1,500 riders, amateur and professional, took part, coming from all over the world. The American team took twice as many titles as any other, with Britain second, and Australia and Holland joint third. Races were held for every age group from 6 to 16, and for the over-17s.

Triathlon

This, the final type of cycle racing isn't really cycle racing at all, but the ultimate test of endurance and stamina. It only began in 1978 and has quickly gained popularity, with thousands of competitors entering triathlon races for titles such as 'the ironman of Hawaii'.

In a full triathlon, you have to swim 4 kilometres (2·4 miles); then cycle a time trial of almost 200 kilometres (112 miles), and finish with a full marathon run (26·2 miles). Only the strongest and fittest need apply, although mini-triathlons are also held, with more manageable distances.

How to start racing

Perhaps cycle racing, with its many types of events, special clothing, special bicycles and special feeding, seems complicated. Well, it needn't be, because racing, in whatever kind of cycling event, is basically about people getting on bicycles and trying to ride faster than their rivals. And that's how you approach cycle racing as a beginner.

You've got a bicycle, maybe a real racing bicycle. So how do you start to race?

The first step is to join a club. There are so many that you shouldn't have to ride far to find one.

There won't be much to pay. Most clubs have very low subscriptions for younger members, and a racing licence (needed for road and track racing but not for time-trials or cyclo-cross) comes automatically in Britain with membership of the British Cycling Federation.

When you join a cycling club you will meet people of all ages and from all walks of life who have an interest in common with you: cycling. The quickest way to learn practical cycling, from maintenance to racing tactics, is to listen to experienced club members. Many clubs have one or more members who are qualified coaches. And if a club doesn't have a coach, then they'll at least be able to introduce you to a local coach.

Don't expect to become a racing star overnight. The first step is to get used to riding your bicycle safely in company. So go on the weekly club runs, where you'll be riding alongside experienced cyclists who'll tell you if and where you're going wrong.

As you get more confident and more used to riding your bicycle fast, you may start to find that you have a talent for a particular type of riding. You may have a good sprint, or hill climbs may seem easy to you.

When this happens, you might easily start thinking (or be persuaded by your friends) that you're going to be a world-beating sprinter or hill climber. Do yourself a favour and don't suddenly start to specialize. Ta-

▷ Two road racing cyclists ready for action, wearing racing jerseys, shorts and special shoes. Note the lightweight crash hat, usually compulsory for track and road racing.

▷ Taking a drink on the run. Feeding bottles can be carried in special 'cages' attached to the bicycle.

lents which appear in early or mid-teens can easily disappear and be replaced by others, as you mature physically and grow stronger. It's not unusual for a fast young track rider to turn into a tough roadman by the time he or she becomes a senior.

So while you're young, try as many different types of racing as you can, and enjoy yourself while you're doing it. You won't harm your chances of being a specialist later by starting as a rider who is ready to tackle anything and everything.

Training

So how do you start training for cycle racing?

This question was once asked of the great Italian champion Fausto Coppi. 'Ride a bike, ride a bike, ride a bike' was his immediate answer. It's a simple message worth remembering. Of course there are scientific training methods, but these cannot be employed until you are basically fit and physically mature.

Start by riding your bicycle as often as you can. But don't be stupid and attempt to cover a greater distance than is comfortable for you. An experienced cyclist will reel off 100 kilometres (over 60 miles) in four hours of 'easy' riding. That same 100 kilometres might take six hours of hard work by a youngster.

One way of making sure that you don't overdo things is by keeping your gears down when you're training. That way you conserve your strength and learn how to pedal fast, an essential for your riding later on.

△ Cold weather shouldn't deter you from training if you are serious about racing.

▷ Before you start racing, seek the help of older, wiser clubmates.

Young riders may not be as strong as their elders, but they have a natural ability to move their limbs fast, so they should find fast pedalling easy. Once learned as a young rider, the ability to pedal fast can be kept for most of your cycling life. If you learn using big gears, relying on strength instead of suppleness, then you'll never be able to pedal any kind of gear fast, and won't be able to pedal a big gear fast in very favourable conditions.

The British Cycling Federation (and many other national governing bodies) recognize this, and have put gear restrictions on track and road races, for schoolboys and girls and juniors. There are no restrictions on gears for time trials, but common sense (and advice from club mates)

should keep your gears down. Whether you're racing or training, you should be pedalling at between 80 and 110 revs per minute, so gear accordingly, and check your revs until you get the 'feel' of the right pedalling rate.

You needn't worry too much about training while you're still at school, because you'll almost certainly be fairly active, and enjoying other sports which will help your basic fitness.

Don't worry about swimming, running, squash or any strenuous sport harming your cycling. It won't and it will almost certainly help. Ride your bicycle as regularly as possible, learn all the time, and enjoy yourself.

When you've been riding for a year or two, and you're maybe 16 or 17 years old, then you can

◁ Taking corners fast will gain you ground, so the techniques are worth practising.

<1 Well dressed for winter training. Note that almost every rider wears a warm hat and gloves.

think about a real training programme.

Here's the basic outline. In the winter ride your bicycle steadily. Go weight training to work on the less developed parts of your body (usually the arms and shoulders with cyclists). Try circuit training (a testing series of exercises in the gymnasium).

Once Christmas is past, increase your riding, but keep the pace steady. Only when the weather starts to get warmer should you be riding flat out during training. And only when you're racing well should you inject the final ingredient, which is interval training; all-out efforts interspersed with rest periods, designed to build up the heart. Interval training isn't right for the developing youngster, however.

If you can't train as hard as your older club mates, you can certainly concentrate on something which is every bit as important – technique. This is always important.

Learn to take corners well, to gauge your strength when riding up hills, to use the right gears for the right occasion. Learn how to place yourself in a group to get the maximum shelter from the wind, to ride close behind another rider but not so close that you're in trouble if he slows down suddenly.

Get to know your bicycle, so any manoeuvre is almost second nature. When you reach that stage, and not before, you can start to think about racing. There's no hurry to start because you can race happily for years.

FAMOUS RACES

When you consider that cycle racing has been a flourishing sport for more than a century, it's not surprising that many current racing events all over the world have a long and eventful history.

Over the years the international calendar, both for amateurs and professionals, has developed with several high points, namely the 'classics', the big tours, and the world championships.

World championships

Let's look at the world championships first. They are held every year, and date back to 1893, when Chicago hosted the first world series, just an amateur sprint and an amateur motor-paced race. An international governing body awards the promotion of the championships two years in advance to candidate countries.

The programme has gradually expanded over the years, and now there are the following events: Amateur:- sprint, tandem sprint, kilometre, points race, individual pursuit, team pursuit, motor-paced, road race and 100 kilometre four-man team time trial. Professional:- sprint, individual pursuit, motor-paced,

Start of a world professional road championship race.

road race. Women:- sprint, individual pursuit, road race.

There are also world championships for juniors (under 19 years) held every year, plus world amateur and professional cyclocross championships, which are held during the winter.

Cycling is an Olympic sport too, and every Olympiad there are medals for sprint, individual and team pursuit, kilometre, team time trial and road race. In Olympic years world champion-ships in these events are not held.

The world championships are generally held towards the end of August, and are naturally a big target for the professionals, whose contract fees and appearance money can be boosted by a good world performance.

Before that, most of the top professional road riders will have ridden in the Tour de France, probably the most famous cycle race in the world; possibly the most famous race in any sport.

△ The magnificent indoor wooden track used for the 1976 Olympics in Montreal. A sprint match is in progress.

Tour de France

The Tour de France is a massive stage race, lasting just over three weeks, and usually including two rest days. Despite its name, the race often moves outside the French frontiers, and in the past has made excursions into Belgium, Holland, Spain, Luxembourg, Switzerland, West Germany and Italy – and in 1974 it even spent one day in Britain.

After a stage in Brittany, the north-west corner of France, the riders were flown over by French military planes to Exeter airport, then went by coach to Plymouth, where a circuit race was held the following day. All the race following vehicles came across by ferry from Roscoff to Plymouth.

The Tour is contested nowadays by 'trade' teams, sponsored by companies whose products vary greatly, from televisions to sausages, from kitchen equipment to department stores. In the past, national teams took part, but problems came about because a trade team rider found it impossible to change loyalties and ride for a national team just in this race, often against his team-mates for the rest of the year.

The Tour de France is big business. It is seen on television screens all over Europe, and Continental newspapers give it enormous coverage. Because of this great attention by the media the Tour can attract all kinds of financial backing. For the privilege of being the start or finish point of a stage, towns pay enormous sums to the organizers, then reap the benefit in increased trade from the thousands who flock to see the race. You can imagine how important such publicity can be to a new winter sports or seaside resort, needing to make its name familiar to the public.

The route is closed to non-race traffic hours beforehand, but such is the enthusiasm of spectators that thousands will walk long distances and up mountain passes to get a good vantage point, taking with them picnic baskets and transistor radios.

The radio tells them how close the race is, but they have other warnings too. Preceding the first race vehicles there is a 'publicity convoy' with vehicles advertising a variety of products and distributing leaflets and souvenirs, loudspeakers blaring.

Then comes the television helicopter, giving its overhead view of the race. Motorcycle policemen shepherd spectators out of the way, as the first of the race cars come through, always in touch with events via 'Radio Tour', a short-wave commentary for press and officials.

The leading riders are surrounded by the buzzing motorcycles of police, mobile television cameramen, and press photographers. Whistles blast a warning message to anyone who, incredibly, might not realize what's happening, and then the race is passing, first the leaders then the 'pack', with each group of riders followed by team cars carrying spare bicycles and wheels.

After the last rider has passed, more police outriders declare the road open, and there's a scramble for parked cars – either to get a good place in the inevitable traffic jam, or to try a short cut and get another quick sight of the race before the day's finish.

And even after the day's pedalling is over, it's still very much Tour time in the stage town, with open-air cabaret (including a film of the day's racing) and the streets filled with celebrating fans.

That's the Tour de France nowadays, but way back in 1903, it was a different story. The Tour was the brainchild of Henri Desgranges, who staged the first event to publicize his newspaper, called l'Auto. The first Tour didn't last three weeks, but instead of riding an average 160 kilometres (100 miles) every day, those early stalwarts would sometimes have to ride 480 kilometres (300 miles). First winner of the Tour was a Frenchman called Maurice Garin, who won the first stage and held the overall lead to the finish.

Those early Tours were tough. The rule was that the rider had to reach the finish unaided – as runner-up in 1912 Eugene Christophe discovered when he broke his front forks.

He had to walk to the nearest village and repair his forks at the local smithy – any help from the blacksmith would have meant disqualification.

On several occasions since, top riders have abandoned the race because they feared bodily harm from over-enthusiastic fans.

This hasn't happened in recent years however, but the Tour has caught the public imagination in other ways. On one memorable occasion President de Gaulle of France greeted the Tour stars when the race passed through his home village; a 'truce' was declared for long enough to introduce the President to the Tour's top names. And the race has become 'fair game' for demonstrators. One way to draw

The 'pack' rounds a hairpin bend in the south of France, halfway on the long road to Paris.

Supporting team cars follow every big cycle race, such as the Tour de France. They carry spare wheels and bicycles for a 'quick change'.

Racing over mountain passes brings changes in temperature. The leading rider here is putting a newspaper up his jersey for warmth before a descent.

Preceding the Tour de France is an eye-catching publicity caravan.

Motor cyclists clear the road and escort the cyclists.

attention to a grievance is to stage a sit-in on the route.

While the main Tour is going on, a women's race is held over a similar course, though with nothing like the same publicity. Other countries have their own equivalents of the Tour de France. Spain has its 'Vuelta'. Italy has its 'Giro'. Smaller national events include the Tours of Switzerland, Holland and Belgium.

Amateur stage races

Amateur racing has its major stage races too. The most famous is the 'Peace Race', run between Warsaw, East Berlin and Prague, with 20 national teams usually competing.

Britain has its own international stage race for amateurs. First run in 1951, it has been sponsored since 1958 by the Milk Marketing Board. Originally called simply the Tour of Britain, it adopted 'The Milk Race' as its title.

The Milk Race is much smaller than the Tour de France, and

until recently only amateur riders were allowed to compete in it. But it owes much to the big French race, with the same town to town structure, the following team cars, the crowds at stage finishes. And it's still an event needing detailed organization; police cooperation so that every junction is marshalled; hotels booked for riders and officials; the route marked with distinctive

△ The triathlete has no time to change, so wears a single suit for swimming, running and cycling.

◁ The world's biggest amateur race, the Peace Race.

Britain's Milk Race, tackling a tricky section.

arrows hours beforehand, with a 'de-routeing' operation to take down the arrows afterwards; and special food for during and after the racing.

Classics

Not all big cycle races have to last several days. In the spring and autumn the calendar is dotted with 'classics' – single-day events which, by virtue of their course and the quality of the field they always attract, are targets for every ambitious cyclist.

One of the most famous of these runs is from Paris (starting from a suburb in the north of the French capital) to Roubaix, a town near the Belgian border.

When the race was first run, in 1896, the roads were far from smooth. Especially towards the end of the course, around the many mining villages which are still there today, the surfaces became very rough, with rutted cobbles, mud and coal-dust transforming the riders into grimy ghostly figures.

The organizers of Paris-Roubaix have tried to keep the character of the race unchanged. Although the main roads to Roubaix are fine, the race now goes via secondary roads, often little better than tracks, and so narrow that following cars are sometimes forced into roadside ditches when riders make sudden moves across the road, searching for a smooth path.

The cobbles are still there, discovered by the energetic route-planners – who have been accused of digging a few ruts of their own when the chosen road is too smooth!

France's other remarkable classic is Bordeaux-Paris, otherwise known as the 'Derby of the Road'. It's about 560 kilometres (350 miles) from Bordeaux to Paris, but the riders – usually only a dozen or so nowadays – are helped by being paced for more than half the distance by small motorcycles, which cut down the effort by sheltering riders from the wind. Bordeaux-Paris started in 1891, and that first race was won by a Briton, George Pilkington Mills, who was paced by teams of other cyclists, and averaged over 20 kph (13 mph) for the distance – about half the current winning speed.

Italy's classics include Milan-San Remo, from the cathedral city to the Italian Riviera.

Belgium is renowned for its flat, windswept roads, and these figure in the Ghent-Wevelgem race. The Ardennes hills, in the South of Belgium, give the biggest problems to riders in the Flèche Wallonne.

Most of the modern classics date back to the beginning of the century. The roads may have changed, the conditions and bicycles have certainly improved, but the character of the racing is still the same: the world's toughest road riders battling to establish supremacy.

Of course not every young cyclist will turn into a Tour de France winner, or the man who comes first out of the 'Hell of the North' into Roubaix. But these great events can inspire even the most inexperienced of racing cyclists to aim higher.

Cobbles and rough roads are a feature of the French Paris-Roubaix classic.

Eddy Merckx of Belgium, the greatest rider of modern times, retired in 1978.

Frenchman Bernard Hinault, a Tour de France winner and good classic rider.

Sean Kelly, the Irish road-racing star of the 1980s.

Francesco Moser of Italy has won a world title on road and track.

Greg Lemond was the first American to win the Tour de France, in 1986.

GLOSSARY

Anatomical saddle
Saddle, probably plastic, designed to provide padding to match the shape of the pelvis; different designs are available for men and women.

Block
The collection of five to seven chainwheels mounted together on the *freewheel* of a *derailleur* cycle.

Bottom bracket
The axle on which the *chainset* and pedal cranks are mounted, sited at the bottom of the *seat tube*.

Cadence
The rate and rhythm at which the pedals are turned; a smooth and reasonably fast cadence is essential for riding with a minimum of effort.

Cage
Device attached to one of the tubes or handlebars, in which a waterbottle may be carried.

Caliper brakes
Any brake system that operates by squeezing the rim between two brake blocks (as opposed to disc or hub brakes).

Cantilever brakes
Type of brakes usually found on tandems or all-terrain cycles, in which the brakes are pivoted on the forms or seat *stays*.

Chainset
The *bottom bracket* and front chainwheel.

Cotterpin
Metal pin sometimes used to secure the pedal crank to the *bottom bracket* axle. Most modern bicycles have a cotterless design.

Derailleur
Gearing mechanism in which the chain is 'derailled' onto chainwheels of varying sizes to effect changes in gear. Derailleurs are used for both front and rear changers.

Dishing
Offsetting the hub of the rear wheel to allow correct alignment of the *block*.

Down tube
The tube of the frame extending from the head tube to the *bottom bracket*.

Dropouts
The flanges attached to the stays and forks, within which the hubs are seated.

Fixed wheel
Removal of the *freewheel* mechanism such that the pedals and wheels turn together.

Forks
The extensions of the *headset*, on which the front wheel is mounted.

Freewheel
The device, to which the *block* may be mounted, that allows the rear wheel to turn without moving the pedals.

Gear ratio
The relationship between the rotation of the pedals and that of the wheel rims, determined by the number of teeth on the front and rear sprockets. A gear ratio chart is shown opposite.

Headset
The assembly where the *forks* and handlebars turn within the head tube.

Hub gear
Type of gear (usually offering three or four gears) incorporating a 'sun-and-planet' system within the hub of the rear wheel.

Jockey wheels
Two small wheels through which the chain threads on a *derailleur* system before being passed onto the rear chainwheels. The jockey wheels are fitted on a sprung arm, and take up any slack as the chain moves from gear to gear.

QR hubs
Hubs fitted with quick release levers, enabling the wheels to be removed by the throw of a lever, rather than by means of a spanner.

Safety levers
Levers attached to brakes on some drop-handlebar cycles, allowing the brakes to

be used while the hands are on the top of the bars. These are rarely as safe as the name implies.

Seat Tube
The main tube of the frame extending from the saddle to the *bottom bracket*.

Sprints
Narrow-section wheels, usually used with *tubular tyres*.

Stays
The thinner tubes of the frame, to which the rear wheel attaches.

Stem
The device that links the handlebars to the *headset* assembly.

Tubular tyres
Single-thickness tyres, used mainly for racing.

Wire-ons
Tyres used for everyday purposes, held on by wires that fit under the rim of the wheel.

USEFUL ADDRESSES

International
Alliance Internationale de Tourisme
Quai Gustave Ador 2.
CH – 1207 Geneva, Switzerland
This is the international federation of touring clubs and motoring associations. Its aim is to promote all forms of international tourism, and it has a special department to look after the interests of cyclists.
Union Cycliste Internationale
8 Rue Charles-Humbert,
1206 Geneva, Switzerland
This is the international controlling body for cycle racing.
Fédération Internationale de Cyclisme (FIAC)
Viale Tiziano
00100 Rome, Italy
Fédération Internationale de Cyclisme Professionel (ACP)
26 Rue de Cessange,
Leudelange, Luxembourg

Australia
Australian Amateur Cyclists Association
40 Gerrale Street, Cronulla 2230, Sydney, NSW, Australia
Australian Cycling Council
153 The Kingsway, Cronulla 2230, Sydney, NSW, Australia

Austria
Österreichischer Radsport Verband
Prinz Eugenstrasse 12, 1040 Vienna, Austria

Belgium
Ligue Vélocipédique Belge
Avenue de Globe 49, Brussels 1190, Belgium
Touring Club Royal de Belgique
Rue de La Loi 44, 1040 Brussels, Belgium

Canada
Association Cycliste Canadienne
333 River Road, Vanier Ottawa, Ontario, Canada
Fédération Cylotouriste Provinciale
4305 Bossuet, Montreal 431, Quebec, Canada

Denmark
Danmarks Cykle Union
Idraettens Hus, 2600 Glostrup, Denmark
Dansk Professionelt Cykle Forbund
Beyerholm Brannersvej 1B, 2920 Charlottenlund, Copenhagen, Denmark

Eire
Irish Cycling Federation
9 Casement Park, Finlas West, Dublin 11, Ireland

France
Fédération Française de Cyclisme
43 Rue de Dunkerque, Paris 10, France
Fédération Française de Cyclotourisme
8 Rue Jean-Marie Jégo, 75013, Paris, France
Touring Club de France
65 Avenue de la Grande-Armée, Paris 16, France
Union des Audax Francais,
5 Rue de Roses, 75018, Paris, France

Germany (East)
Deutscher Radsport Verband
Storkowerstrasse 118, 1055 Berlin, East Germany

Germany (West)
Bund Deutscher Radfahrer
Otto-Fleck-Schneise 4, 6000 Frankfurt, West Germany

Italy
Federazione Ciclistica Italiana
Viale Tiziano 70, 00100 Rome, Italy
Touring Club Italiano
Corso Italia 10, 20122 Milan, Italy

Jamaica
The Jamaica Amateur Cycling Association
6 Simmons Close, 6 Kingstone, Jamaica

Japan
Japan Amateur Cycling Federation
Kishi Memorial Hall, 1-1-1 Jinnan, Shibuyaku, Tokyo, Japan
Fédération Japonaise de Cyclisme Professionel

9-15 Akasake, 1 Chome Minato Ku,
Tokyo, Japan
Luxembourg
*Fédération du Sport Cycliste
Luxembourgeois*
Case Postale 2253, Luxembourg Ville,
Luxembourg
Netherlands
Royal Dutch Touring Club
Wassenaarsweg 220, The Hague,
Netherlands
Koninklijke Nederlandsche Wieleren Unie
15 Nieuwe Uitleg, The Hague,
Netherlands
Netherlands Cycletouring Union
Ambactsherenlaaw 1162A, 2722-VJ-
Zoetermeer, Netherlands
New Zealand
*New Zealand Amateur Cycling
Association*
P.O. Box 3104, Wellington, New Zealand
Norway
Norges Cykleforbund
Hauger Skolevei 1-1346 Gjettum, Oslo 1,
Norway
Portugal
Federacao Portuguesa de Ciclismo
Rua Barros Queiroz 39-10, Lisbon,
Portugal
Spain
Federacion Espanola de Ciclismo
Ferraz 16-50, Madrid 8, Spain
Switzerland
Union Cycliste Suisse,
4 Rue de Vieux-College, 1211, Geneva 3,
Switzerland
United Kingdom
Audax (UK)
188 Runcorn Road, Moore, Warrington
WA4 6SY
(Organizes long distance rides.)
Bike Events
41 Floral Street, London WC2
(Organizes London to Brighton ride and
other mass rides.)
British Cycling Federation
70 Brompton Road, London SW3 1EN

(The British governing body for cycle
racing on road and track).
British Cyclo-Cross Association
8 Bellam Road, Hampton Magna, Near
Warwick, Warwickshire
British Triathlon Association
3 Porters Avenue, Dagenham, Essex RM9
5YS
Cyclists' Touring Club
Cotterell House, Meadrow, Godalming,
Surrey
Northern Ireland Cycling Federation
9A Great Northern Street, Belfast,
Northern Ireland
Road Records Association
100 Betham Road, Greenford, Middlesex
UB6 8SA
Road Time Trials Council
Dallacre, Mill Road, Yarwell,
Peterborough PE8 6PS
*Royal Society for the Prevention of
Accidents*
Cannon House, The Priory, Queensway,
Birmingham B4 6BS
(Administers the National Cycling
Proficiency Scheme.)
Scottish Cyclists' Union
293 Rosemount Place, Aberdeen, Scotland
UKBMX
74 Cuxton Road, Strood, Kent ME2 2BU
The Youth Hostels Association
Trevelyan House, 8 St Stephens Hill, St
Albans, Hertfordshire AL1 2DY
*The Youth Hostels Association Travel
and Services Department*
29 John Adam Street, London WC2
United States of America
United States Cycling Federation
1385 Graham Street,
53151 New Berlin, Wisconsin, USA
League of American Wheelmen (Touring)
19 South Bothwell Street, Palatine, Illinois
60067, USA
Professional Racing Organisation USA
310 Olly Street, 80220 Denver, Colorado,
USA

INDEX

Numbers in **bold** refer to illustrations.